Burgoyne

SURROUNDED

New Quilts from an Old Favorite

edited by
Linda Baxter Lasco

THANK YOU SPONSORS

Clover

✳️ Fairfield
Quality Polyester Products for Home and Industry

JANOME
Because You Simply Love To Sew™

Located in Paducah, Kentucky, the American Quilter's Society (AQS) is dedicated to promoting the accomplishments of today's quilters. Through its publications and events, AQS strives to honor today's quiltmakers and their work and to inspire future creativity and innovation in quiltmaking.

Executive Book Editor: Andi Milam Reynolds
Senior Editor: Linda Baxter Lasco
Graphic Design: Lynda Smith
Cover Design: Michael Buckingham
Photography: Charles R. Lynch

American Quilter's Society
P. O. Box 3290 ï Paducah, KY 42002-3290
www.americanquilter.com

Library of Congress Cataloging-in-Publication Data

Burgoyne surrounded : new quilts from an old favorite / by American Quilter's Society.
    p. cm. -- (New quilts from an old favorite)
  ISBN 978-1-57432-981-0
  1. Burgoyne surrounded quilts. 2. Quilting--Competitions--United States. I. American Quilter's Society.

 NK9112.A5385 2009
 746.46079'73--dc22

                    2009002137

Additional copies of this book may be ordered from the American Quilter's Society, PO Box 3290, Paducah, KY 42002-3290, or online at www.AmericanQuilter.com.

Proudly printed and bound in the
United States of America

DEDICATION

This book is dedicated to all those who see a traditional quilt block and can visualize both its link to the past and its bridge to the future.

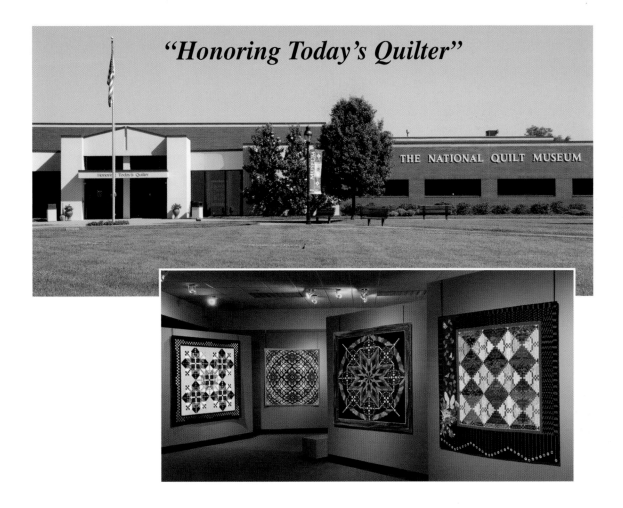

The National Quilt Museum (NQM) is an exciting place where the public can learn more about quilts, quiltmaking, and quiltmakers, and experience quilts that inspire and delight.

The museum celebrates today's quilts and quiltmakers through exhibits of quilts from the museum's collection and selected temporary exhibits. By providing a variety of workshops and other programs, NQM helps to encourage, inspire, and enhance the development of today's quilter.

Whether presenting new or antique quilts, the museum promotes understanding of and respect for all quilts—new and antique, traditional and innovative, machine made and handmade, utility and art.

CONTENTS

BURGOYNE SURROUNDED: New Quilts from an Old Favorite

PREFACE

While preservation of the past is one of a museum's primary functions, its greatest service is performed as it links the past to the present and to the future. With that intention, The National Quilt Museum sponsors an annual contest and exhibit called New Quilts from an Old Favorite (NQOF).

Created to acknowledge our quiltmaking heritage and to recognize innovation, creativity, and excellence, the contest challenges today's quiltmakers to interpret a single traditional quilt block in a work of their own design. Each year contestants respond with a myriad of stunning interpretations.

Burgoyne Surrounded: New Quilts from an Old Favorite is a wonderful collection of these interpretations. You'll find a brief description of the 2009 contest, followed by a presentation of the five award winners and 13 finalists and their quilts.

Full-color photographs of the quilts accompany each quiltmaker's comments—comments that provide insight into their widely diverse creative processes. A pattern for the traditional Burgoyne Surrounded block is included to give you a starting point for your own rendition. The winners and finalists' tips, techniques, and patterns offer an artistic framework for your own work.

Our wish is that *Burgoyne Surrounded: New Quilts from an Old Favorite* will further our quiltmaking heritage as new quilts based on the Burgoyne Surrounded block are inspired by the outstanding quilts in this book.

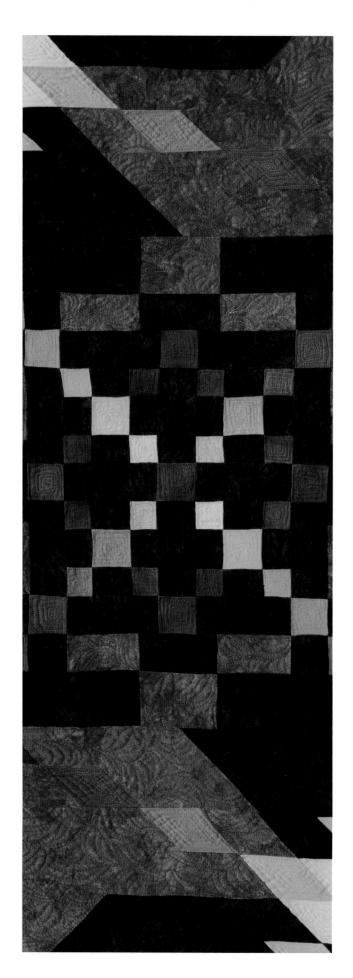

THE CONTEST

The New Quilts from an Old Favorite contest requires that quilts entered be recognizable in some way as a variation of the selected traditional block. The quilts must be no larger than 80" and no smaller than 50" on a side. Each quilt entered must be quilted. Quilts may only be entered by the maker(s) and must have been completed after December 31 two years prior to the entry date.

Quiltmakers are asked to send in two images—one of the full quilt and one detail shot—for jurying. Three jurors view these and consider technique, artistry, and interpretation of the theme block to select finalists from among all the entries. These finalist quilts are then sent to the museum where a panel of three judges carefully evaluates them. The evaluation of the actual quilts focuses on design, innovation, theme, and workmanship. The first-through fifth-place winners are selected and notified.

An exhibit of all the winning and finalist quilts opens at The National Quilt Museum in Paducah each spring, then travels to venues around the country for two years. Thousands of quilt lovers have enjoyed these exhibits nationwide.

A book is produced by the American Quilter's Society featuring full-color photos of the finalist and award-winning quilts, biographical information about each quilter, and tips, techniques, and patterns. The book provides an inside look at how quilts are created and a glimpse into the artistic mindset of today's quilters.

Previous theme blocks have been Double Wedding Ring, Log Cabin, Kaleidoscope, Mariner's Compass, Ohio Star, Pineapple, Storm at Sea, Bear's Paw, Tumbling Blocks, Feathered Star, Monkey Wrench, Seven Sisters, Dresden Plate, Rose of Sharon, and Sawtooth. The Sunflower block has been selected for the 2010 contest. Orange Peel, Baskets, and Jacob's Ladder will be the featured blocks for 2011 through 2013.

NQM would like to thank this year's sponsors: Fairfield Processing Corporation; Janome America, Inc.; and Clover Needlecraft, Inc.

BURGOYNE SURROUNDED BLOCK

Who—or what—was Burgoyne? Why does this name title a quilt block? Without diary entries or letters to examine, we can only speculate, but we can look at possible reasons suggested by the period of the block's popularity and the colors used for Burgoyne Surrounded quilts.

The American victory in 1777 over General John Burgoyne at Saratoga, New York, was a major factor in the American Revolution, convincing France to enter the war. As the United States began its second century of existence, celebrating and evoking momentous events of the Revolution and our colonial past became a trend in American life. We refer to this as the colonial revival and it grew in earnest after the Philadelphia Centennial Exposition of 1876. An event such as a decisive American Revolutionary War victory would be a perfect topic for depiction in the revival.

The *Ohio Farmer* published a pattern named Beauregard's Surroundings around 1890, and in 1897 the Ladies Art Company of St. Louis published pattern #285 titled An Old Patchwork. Visually these are the same as the pattern we know today as Burgoyne Surrounded that was published around 1930 by *Household Magazine*. The same pattern was called Burgoyne's Puzzle by *Home Art* in the 1930s and Coverlet Quilt by *Capper's Weekly* (no date). Depending on the sashing design, the same block has been named The Road to California, Wheel of Fortune, Homespun, Burgoyne's Quilt (specifically with red, white, and blue fabrics), and Burgoyne Surrounded.

An online search for Burgoyne Surrounded quilts yielded eight from the Quilt Index (www.quiltindex.org) and three from the collection of the International Quilt Study Center & Museum (www.quiltstudy.org). These eleven quilts date from as far back as 1865 to as recent as the 1970s. The quilt dated 1865 is made of navy fabrics for the design and white background fabrics; two quilts with no date also follow this color plan. A quilt from 1890 and the two from 1900 to 1929 are made of red fabrics for the pattern and white or white shirting for the background. A 1930–1950 quilt is pieced of green fabrics for the pattern and white for the background; the green looks to be a typical Nile green of the Depression. One quilt, made by Mary Shafer in 1974, follows the red, white, and blue scheme noted above. Only one of the quilts is in three colors plus white, a 1935–1945 quilt. The remaining quilts had indeterminate color schemes.

Two-color quilts were popular in the 1840s and 1850s, but typically they were of colorfast Turkey red prints with white background fabrics. The expanses of white fabric were perfect for the wreaths, feathers, and other ornate quilting of the mid-nineteenth century. Indigo, long noted for its colorfastness, has been used for two-color quilts practically since the craft began. An article in the 1898 issue of *The Modern Priscilla* noted a "pretty indigo blue and white print and white muslin combine beauty with the coveted old-time air more effectively than any style of cotton patchwork." Stearns and Foster copyrighted a pattern in 1932, #34 in the Mountain Mist series, calling it Homespun, and suggested it be pieced in red and white.

This would all suggest that two-color Burgoyne Surrounded quilts from 1880 to about 1910 would be the norm. As seven of these study quilts were made after 1900, it would appear that the popularity of the Burgoyne Surrounded pattern came later than the published patterns and literature would suggest, but making the quilt in two colors holds true. Clearly this was a colonial revival pattern, yet it appears to have been most popular during the Depression era, when the first quilt revival of the twentieth century began. The three quilts made after 1950 suggest that the simplicity of the pattern—all straight line piecing of simple squares and rectangles—made it a perfect pattern for the beginning of the second quilt revival of the twentieth century. With the advent of the rotary cutter and strip-piecing methods, the old favorite was once again a popular pattern.

Judy Schwender
Paducah, Kentucky
January 2, 2009

Brackman, Barbara, *Encyclopedia of Pieced Quilt Patterns* (American Quilter's Society: Paducah, KY) 1993. Katherine B. Johnson, "New Ideas in Patchwork," *The Modern Priscilla*, May 1898, p. 7, in *The American Quilt: A History of Cloth and Comfort* 1750-1950, Roderick Kiracofe (Clarkson Potter: New York) 1993.

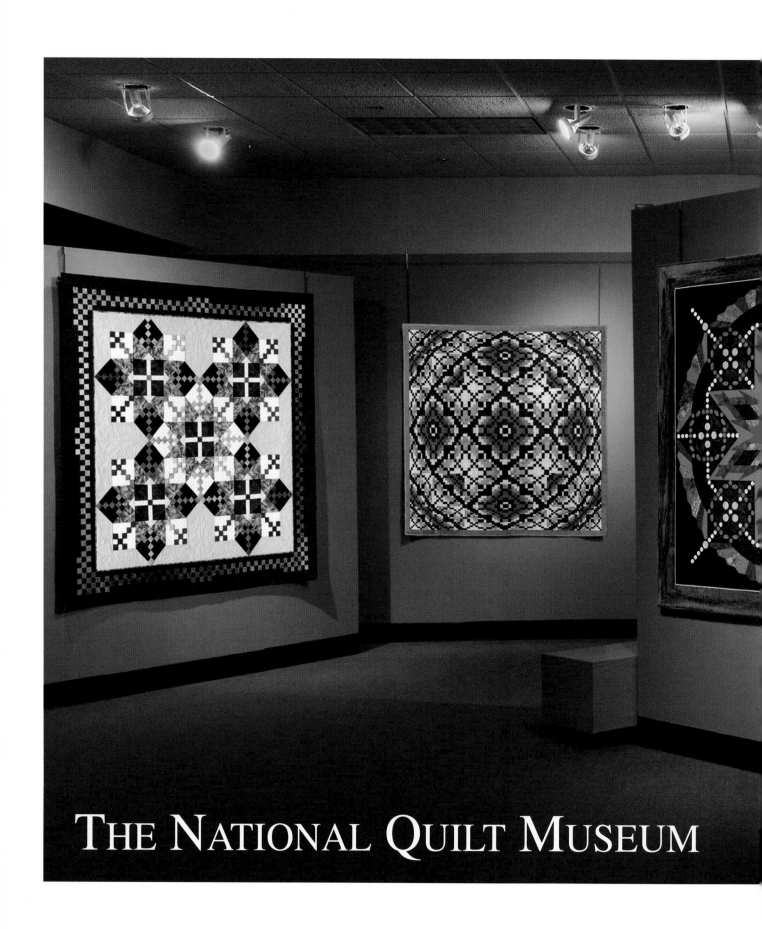

THE NATIONAL QUILT MUSEUM

BURGOYNE SURROUNDED: New Quilts from an Old Favorite

The National Quilt Museum
215 Jefferson Street • Paducah, Kentucky 42001 • www.quiltmuseum.org • (270) 442-8856

Photo by Madhu Malik

Cathryn Zeleny
Yountville, California

Meet the Quilter

By the mid 1990s, I had been a "professional" painter/art-ist for most of my adult life. I had exhibited in numerous local, regional, and national art shows and competitions, and had won awards. My work had been carried by galler-ies and I sold a few paintings each year. However, I was not making my living as an artist! I always had to work at a "real" job in order to pay the bills. Needless to say, I was dissatisfied with the lack of progress in my chosen career.

In 1997, I had a bad year. First, I was diagnosed with glau-coma and second, I was seriously injured at work. Shortly thereafter, I lost my job and my home, and then both my dog and my father-in-law died. It was a difficult time and I spent most of the next year in a weird, hazy fog of either pain or medication to control the pain. Sometimes, though, when bad things happen to us, good can come from it. Along with enforced inactivity comes the opportunity for introspection.

I keep photographic slides of all the art that I have ever made. I went through them and pulled out 66 slides, each of a painting I had done of the nude female figure. It did not take me long to realize that there were only four that I would hang on my own walls! The remaining 62 were nothing more than rote exercises in painting the female figure that could have been done by any artist. They did not say "I am a Cathryn Zeleny!"

So, I went on a quest. I resolved to find the subject matter that was most meaningful to me, whether in the external world or within myself, around which I could build a mature body of artwork.

As it happens, I got sidetracked. While visiting my mother in July of 1999, I went to my first quilt show. I had sewn

INEVITABLE 54" x 54"

"I went on a quest, resolved to find the subject matter around which I could build a mature body of artwork. As is happens, I got sidetracked."

my entire life, both garments and toys, and had done many other needle arts as well. But I had never been introduced to quiltmaking nor to patchwork and piecing. And I was intrigued. I love jigsaw puzzles, logic puzzles, and even geometry.

I purchased a packet of fat quarters at the show and started designing quilts in my head on the five-hour drive home. It took me 11 days to design and complete my first quilt. It has 60 four-inch blocks, each of which has ten pieces, all with curved seams, that make the blocks look like an ocean wave. I then designed a quilting pattern of curved lines and clamshells, which I did with my zigzag foot because I had not yet heard of free-motion. I guessed at how to do the binding.

The following day I woke up with an idea for my second quilt, and that was it; I was hooked. I started making quilts. All the time. Happily. What I wasn't doing was painting, or making "serious" art. And it felt good.

Inspiration and Design

In 2001, I had an idea for a quilt for the Tumbling Blocks: New Quilts from an Old Favorite contest. I was honored to have my STUMBLING BLOCKS quilt chosen as one of the 18 finalists. I decided that I had to go to Paducah to see my quilt hanging in the museum in the spring of 2002.

Unfortunately, I have this little problem. I am severely claustrophobic. I do not fly. I do not use buses or trains, do bridges or tunnels, elevators or escalators, nor go higher than the third floor of a building! So I decided I had to drive. And if I was going to go all the way to Kentucky, I would continue on to the Atlantic Coast to see family and friends. So, I drove, from California to Maine to North Carolina and back again, in one day less than seven weeks, 10,200 miles, by myself. I had a great trip. I also had my artistic epiphany.

Early one morning, while visiting the Outer Banks of North Carolina, I went to Jockey's Ridge State Park, containing the largest naturally occurring sand dunes east of the Mississippi. I got out of my car and started up the closest dune and walked, straight up, for a long time.

As I got to the top and my eyes crested the dune, I could see the top of the next dune, and then the next, and the next, and then the ocean and the sky. I came to a dead stop and exclaimed in awe, "This is it!" This is what I had been painting for 25 years—three-dimensional, undulating and/or overlapping forms in space, generally rising vertically, visually, toward either heaven or toward outer space. These shapes speak to me on a spiritual or metaphysical level.

It isn't just sand dunes. It's the California hills, ocean waves, snow drifts, the pebbles in a stream, ripples in the sand, the petals of a flower, the arms of a cactus, vegetables in a market, a cityscape, the Pueblo at Taos, or the Roman ruins. It is the human figure: the arm in front of the breast in front of the torso. If you take these subjects and crop them very tightly, leaving only a small portion of the whole so that you can no longer tell what the original source was, then these forms become universal.

When I returned from my trip, I started painting and drawing again. In 2004, following a class with Caryl Bryer Fallert, I made a duplicate of one of my pastel paintings as a quilt. Over the next three years, I made seven large quilts in this series, either from my original paintings or from sketches.

In December of 2007, I checked on the upcoming NQOF contest to see which block had been chosen for 2008. I went online to find out who Burgoyne was and why he would be surrounded. As I was reading about the British general and his surrender at Saratoga, I got a mental picture of hills surrounding a valley. The image soon transformed into a visual metaphor: a topographical map of these undulating and overlapping forms that I had been using since my sand dune revelation, enclosing the Burgoyne Surrounded block.

Thus Burgoyne is surrounded by the circle in the block itself, by the other eight blocks that form the nine-block set of my quilt, by the visually three-dimensional forms that are superimposed on these blocks, and by the contour lines of the channel-stitch quilting that enhances the forms. It is inevitable that he would surrender, as it is inevitable that one of the museum's annual block choices would eventually meld so perfectly with the imagery I am currently exploring.

Technique

In order to create my quilt, I had to superimpose the three-dimensional imagery onto the Burgoyne Surrounded block. I had used a similar technique in three of my previous quilts and have developed a fairly simple way to accomplish this. I use a nine-step value scale. It is the easiest way to break down the light and dark ranges of an apparently round object.

I started with a black-and-white sketch and enlarged it on a value-accurate Xerox® copier (fig. 1).

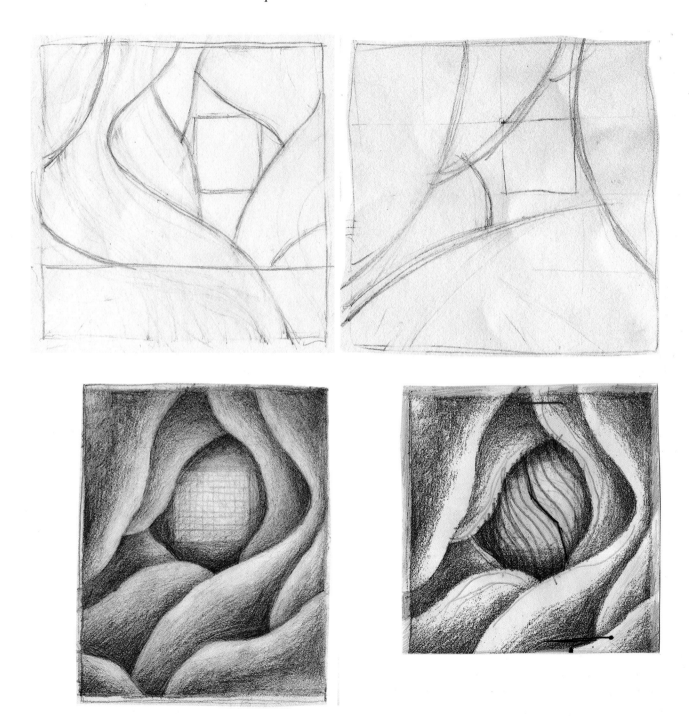

Fig. 1. My original rectangular design was later cropped to a square.

Fig. 2. Nine-step value gradation

Fig. 3. Nine-step value gradation lines copied onto acetate

I used a Sharpie® marker and a contour-type line to divide each form into three sections—light, medium, and dark. Then I divided each subsection into light, medium, and dark. (For example, the lightest section gets divided into a lightest light, a medium light, and a dark light.) This results in a nine-step value gradation that has a smooth transition (fig. 2).

I numbered the sections (1 for the darkest through 9 for the lightest) and copied only the lines onto acetate (fig. 3).

In order to superimpose these form gradations onto Burgoyne Surrounded, I modified the block in to 1" squares using my Electric Quilt® 5 computer program. The entire quilt is a Nine-Patch arrangement of 17" x 17" blocks plus a pieced sashing along the outside edges.

After enlarging the acetate value lines to the same size as the block printout, I taped them together, and used a window to transfer the lines and make the master pattern for piecing (fig. 4, page 15).

I arrange my fabric stash in a nine-step value gradation, rather than by color. In each of the nine values, I picked out approximately 16 black-and-whites to be the 'whites' of the block, and five reds. Each of the forms was pieced as a separate entity, using whole one-inch fabric squares for any pattern square that was partially bisected by the edge of the form. After all the forms were completed, the curved edges were trimmed with a ¼" seam allowance and pressed under. These were topstitched to each other, working from the center out. This was facilitated by having pressed all the pieced seams open, a technique suggested to me by Janet Fogg in the class she teaches at Empty Spools Seminars at Asilomar, California.

The value gradations were enhanced by the quilting. I used a walking foot to quilt parallel lines ⅜" apart on each form in the direction most similar to the value contours (fig. 5). This was done using three different values of threads—again light, medium, and dark. They are matched to the appropriate sections of each form.

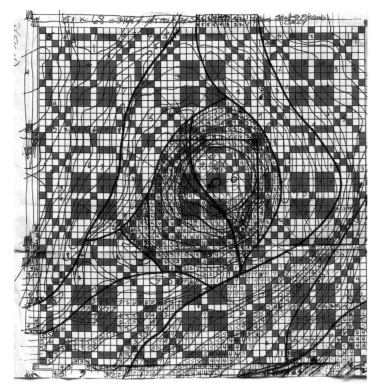

Fig. 4. Master pattern for piecing

Fig. 5. Detail of parallel quilting

Photo by Jessica Horton

Second Place

Ann Horton

Redwood Valley, California

Meet the Quilter

I've always been an artist— even as a little girl, the family knew me to be the one that would draw, paint, sew, and create. Quilting was a natural for me. My grandmothers quilted. My mother sewed our clothes. Living on the farm, this all seemed as normal as tomatoes in the summertime. As a young mother, my diversified interests in all things handmade became focused on quiltmaking, and this continues as a powerful force in my life. A "serious" quilter for the past 25 years (defined by the time I spend at my art as well as the ever-increasing size of my fabric and quilting stash), I spend 20+ hours a week in my studio. I find quilting to be very energizing and therapeutic. I am also a psychotherapist, a musician, and live a country life in Northern California, and these endeavors find their way into my quilt designs. Nature, the celebration of song, the deeply felt emotions of family, relationships, and life—all are fertile ground for my imagination and art.

Another aspect of my life as a quilter is my relationship with my best pals and quilting cohorts. Shared inspiration, new techniques, and the great feeling of laughter and letting off steam are all part of a recipe for grand times of creativity. Our small group of 11 women meets twice a month to indulge in all the whimsy and passion of our shared textile art addiction. After fifteen years together, we know one another well yet surprise ourselves with new discoveries and creative "pushes" every time. Oh the joy of sisterhood!

As is often the case, my family applauds my artistic work. Bless them, they hear my quilting woes, cheer me on, cook and do the dishes, and put up with my frequent disappearances into my studio. My husband's support is ever abundant and I share this with a great deal of gratitude in my heart for all the love that surrounds and supports my work.

I expect this all to continue, of course! New ideas flow readily, with the usual backlog of plans on the drawing table. I love a

PRAYERS OF MY PEOPLE 68" x 68"

"The quilt celebrates the blessings of many places and people as well as our sacred relationship with our Creator."

good challenge and find show deadlines and contests to be incentives for new quilts. Amazing machines, incredible fabrics of all colors and designs, those luscious threads, beads, and embellishments... it all sings to me the siren song of creativity. I am blessed, called to do the work, satisfied that in the end, I have done my best, and lean into the next project with an open mind for more learning.

Inspiration and Design

Burgoyne Surrounded—just the name of that block inspired images of the past. I was certain I would enjoy delving into a historical quilt to do it justice... and then the design took off in an entirely different direction. As I studied the traditional block, I started to play with the idea of rearranging the color.

What if I treated the block like a Log Cabin and split the coloring? Before I could stop myself (forgetting all about the pictorial history quilt I had thought of making), I began pulling fabrics from my stash. As I reached for the many lush, diverse, and richly colored textiles from Asia, Africa, Bali, Australia, Europe, and North and South America, I thought, "This quilt is starting to look like a global stew!"

Why was I leaning toward fabrics from all over the world? I was not sure, but I loved the look. Then my eye fell on my open bin of silk and out came the luscious reds, gold, ivory, and blues. I knew I had to add the silk as my fabric pile grew to over 100 different lights and darks. I redrew the block to make the little squares and rectangles look more circular and pieced my first block. I loved it!

I realized that I would need nine blocks and that I would have to design the layout of fabrics for all the blocks at once. This would help the flow from one block to another, creating the light and shadow I desired for the pieced section of the quilt. That's all I knew at that point, but it was enough. I began the exciting and complicated task of choosing all the right fabrics to carefully craft the color and texture of the piece, fitting in the crisscross of the medium and dark red silks.

Those other silk colors found their way into well-placed positions throughout the quilt. Piecing those tiny red silk squares and rectangles proved to be an immense task, but I persevered until I accomplished what I had envisioned—a richly baroque tapestry of color and shadings. Uncertain where I wanted to take it next, I hung up the lush beauty and just lived with it for a while.

As so often happens, I dreamed the next part of the quilt. I simply awoke one morning and knew I needed words—not just any words but the words of prayers. My husband has written many beautiful prayers for our church worship services and I, too, have written prayers. As the contemporary music director, I also knew song as another rich form of prayer. Phrases and words would hum and float through my head week after week. I wanted to add these prayers to my quilt.

I am adept at machine embroidery and knew my software would allow me to write and design the prayers for embroidering onto the quilt. In the end, sixteen prayers were embroidered into the pieced section of the quilt.

I knew the border needed to inform the viewer of the sacred aspect of the quilt. The embroidered prayers were subtle, so the border needed to suggest prayer. Again I thought of our songs of praise with uplifted hands. I decided to personalize the quilt here with a photo print of my own hands on silk (fig. 1).

Fig. 1. Photo print of hands on silk

The floating rose petals gave the sense of beauty rising, and the tiny shell circle beads would represent the many words. The three embroidered butterflies would represent the Trinity, helping our prayers along their way (fig. 2).

Fig. 2. Floating rose petals

The garden of silk appliqué flowers would "ground" the hands, affording a base from which the prayers would rise. I began by adapting some of Nancy A. Pearson's *Floral Appliqué* (1994) patterns. In the end, I just continued to add more silk flowers until the appliqués had spilled across the border sections to make their statement.

The background fabric for the border was critical for the success of the quilt. Then I knew why I had been drawn to such an array of choices. The quilt was a celebration of the gift of prayer for all people and needed to include the global fabrics. The border was no exception. Again, my stash provided. I pulled out a beautiful, very dark ikat I had purchased for a never-to-be-made jacket. The natural, textured surface of the ikat was a great contrast to the red silks. This ikat was also woven with different sections of design. So many possibilities!

After much consideration, I carefully cut the ikat for maximum effect. The beautiful bottom section of interwoven cream threads would be the base for the shell disks of "prayer beads." The two smaller side weavings would give a beautiful edge for a bit of hand embroidery and quilting, and the one section of tweedy weave would be the background for the silk appliqués. I added another section of the border edging to this area to complete the rhythm of the repeats.

Another very challenging fabric to work with, the soft and textured ikat presented problems and new solutions to get it all to lie well. After searching many shops for the right binding, I came home to the bits of scraps left from the ikat and carefully cut and put together the perfect binding to blend the border edges together.

Technique—It's All in the Details

I would like to invite the reader to take a closer look at PRAYERS OF MY PEOPLE. My quilt design work attempts to include "the big picture" of overall design, composition, and color. I try to think in unusual and unexpected ways. And over and over again, I find myself adding to this mix a great deal of detailed design. This quilt was no exception.

Fig. 3. Embroidery

I approached embroidered lettering by assessing the areas of the quilt that could receive the words. I decided that nine prayers would be written in a circular fashion around the center of each block. Each prayer would have four phrases to fit into the rectangles around the center square. I choose a lovely script font and shaped the writing into a gentle arch (fig. 3).

The thread color was matched to the background print so that it could be read yet not stand out too brightly. More prayers were added horizontally and vertically. The final three prayers were stitched in the outer rectangles of the pieced section, wrapping around the quilt.

The red Guatemalan fabric inner border was applied and hand-quilted in place. After the dark ikat border was added, a small cream cord was couched into place (fig. 4).

The hands were first photographed, then "toned down" in the photo software program, and printed on silk. The silk was backed with soft interfacing, and a very thin layer of polyester batting was added before they were hand appliquéd in place. Hand-quilted lifelines made this a very personal part of the piece. Beading was added beneath the hands to help integrate the image into the quilt (fig. 5).

Most of the hand-appliquéd silk flowers were completed before the border was attached. Some flower details were added later to allow the appliqué to spill

Fig. 4. Red inner border and couched cord

Fig. 5. Beading detail

into the bottom border (fig. 6). The butterflies were also embroidered before the border was attached, and all machine quilting was completed as each border was added. The bottom border includes several embroidered designs in subtle black thread (fig. 7). Additional hand embroidery in the outer border includes small black raised squares and hand-quilted stitches, done with the same thick perle cotton thread used to tie on the shell disks at the bottom. This is another way to integrate and repeat elements throughout the quilt. Tiny circular shell beads were hand sewn among the red petals to repeat the circle shape and shell motif (fig. 8).

A final word about materials is in order. The juxtaposition of silk with cotton, woven ikat, and rough Guatemalan fabric suggests the many faces and textures of the peoples of this earth. Difficult to integrate into one piece, the quilt fabric continues to make a statement about our world and the challenges we face. The beautiful threads tie it together—rayon from Coats & Clark, Sulky, Madeira, and Robinson-Anton live peacefully with the thick cotton DMC threads. Thin silk thread from YLI provides delicate hand quilting on the single rose petals. Finding the right fabric, threads, and embellishments can be a treasure hunt that is a pleasure to experience.

Details draw the viewer into the quilt. While this kind of work takes innovative approaches and a variety of materials, it is also interesting and challenging to undertake. In the end, the quilt celebrates the blessings of many places and people as well as our sacred relationship with our Creator. It was a delight to stitch and an abundant blessing to share.

Fig. 6. Appliqué flower detail

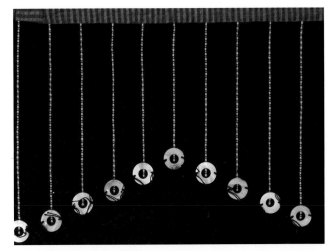

Fig. 7. Bottom border detail

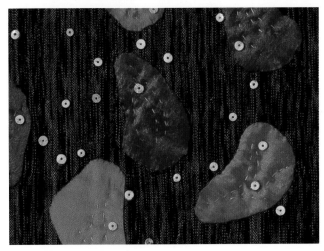

Fig. 8. Circular shell beads

Photo by Mark J. Ferring

Third Place
Karen Watts
Houston, Texas

Meet the Quilter

I've been quilting for about 17 years now and am still fascinated by the variety of pattern, color, and possibilities for expression that exist for a quilter. Over the years I've seen a definite progression in my preferences. When I started quilting, like most beginners I stuck with published patterns and fabrics that were not very adventurous. Before too long I discovered that I really liked scrappy quilts—the bigger variety of fabric used the better! If you need red fabric in a quilt, why not use 20 reds instead of one? Scrappy quilts are such fun to look at. I loved lots of color and chose patterns that had very little or no background at all.

Then I discovered the fun of designing. I started with sets of exchange blocks and tried to do something unique with them. Next I participated in guild and bee challenges and had so much fun I decided to enter the Sawtooth: New Quilts from an Old Favorite contest in 2007. I enjoyed it so much I entered again in 2008 and am already looking forward to the next.

I've always enjoyed every part of the process of quilting— choosing the design and fabrics, the piecing, and the quilting. But, I seemed to pile up tops faster than I could quilt them on my Pfaff, so in 2004 I bought a Gammill longarm. I thought that surely I would catch up on my quilting, and did finally finish many of my completed tops. I also quilt for others, though, so I still have a pile of unquilted tops. Like most quilters, I have many works in progress, otherwise known as UFOs. The oldest one dates from around 1997 but I do intend to finish it someday.

I have two children and stopped working full time in 1992 when my daughter was a baby. I had started quilting right before she was born and fit quilting in whenever I could manage some time between caring for a baby and a four-year-old. When my children were young, quilting was a way to stay connected to the adult world. We moved to Houston in late 1994, and I was thrilled to attend the International Quilt Festival for the first time in 1995. I

MANDALA 66" x 66"

"I bought a Gammill longarm thinking I would catch up on my quilting, but I still have many UFOs."

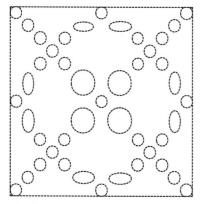

Fig. 1.

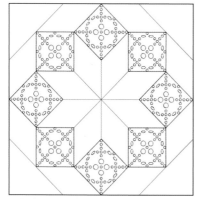

Fig. 2.

Fig. 3.

Fig. 4.

was blown away by the array of fabulous quilts on display and the vendors. I've never been able to attend the Paducah show, but that is definitely on my to-do list. Soon we will transition to the empty-nest phase of life and I'm hoping to be able to do some traveling to many of the major shows across the country.

Inspiration and Design

The Burgoyne Surrounded block has wonderful potential for secondary designs and circular motion. As I was trying out different ways to use the block, I found I really liked designs that emphasized circles. Finally I thought to myself, "What if I made the block itself with circles and ovals instead of squares and rectangles?" I drew the block the traditional way, then drew circles in the colored square areas (non-background) and ovals in the rectangles. Next I removed the piecing lines altogether, which left me with a plain square with circles and ovals on it (fig. 1).

As I experimented with this block in different settings, I discovered an exciting secondary design formed when the Burgoyne blocks were used as setting blocks for a Lone Star (fig. 2). The dots forming the X joined to make a huge octagon, with eight circles intersecting. This had potential. Realizing that I could set any block I wanted into the points of the Lone Star, I started auditioning blocks for the star.

A Churn Dash looked good, but needed some modifications to make it more interesting. When I set the modified Churn Dash into the diamond shape, it reminded me of arrows, which seemed appropriate given the story behind the Burgoyne Surrounded block (fig. 3). I also decided to use a Churn Dash block behind the dots of the Burgoyne Surrounded block, rather than setting them on a plain square.

That turned out to be a good decision, as I could use the piecing lines of the Churn Dash to place the circles for appliqué. Having uniform guidelines allowed me to make the blocks as close to identical as possible (fig. 4).

I needed a block in the outer diamonds that would continue the circular theme, and the Dresden Fan accomplished that nicely. Setting the fans into the diamonds is what turned the quilt into a mandala (fig. 5, page 25).

I didn't decide what to do with the corners until the quilt was mostly pieced together. After appliquéing 360 circles I really wasn't excited about doing more, but it seemed to need a few more extending out to the corners. So I forced myself to make and appliqué 20 more circles.

I found the perfect dark background—not solid, not black, but a rich walnut that looked like old painted wood. Many of the reds and golds came from my stash, but I had to search for the right red fabric for the dots. The one I chose is a wonderful geometric pattern that gives a lot of variety in the pieces when cut up. The dots have unity, but are not boring to look at, as they are not all the same. I didn't want the Burgoyne blocks to be too busy, so I chose a very dark green with highlights of gold for the Churn Dash blocks behind the dots. You have to look a little harder to see that block. The gold fabric with red and green geometric designs in the center "bars" on the star tied it all together. I tried various pieced borders for the quilt, but ultimately decided that would be too busy and let the beautiful Bali fabric speak for itself.

Technique

Appliqué has always been the A word to me. Consequently, when I designed a quilt that needed ANY appliqué, let alone 380 circles and ovals, my friends thought I was nuts. I would not have been able to do it without a handy product called Perfect Circles® templates by Karen Kay Buckley (www. karenkaybuckley.com). Perfect Circles is a set of templar (heat-resistant plastic) washers in 15 different sizes, 4 of each size. Since the washers are templar, they may be ironed without melting.

To make appliqué circles using the washers, cut a circle of fabric the size of your washer plus ¼" seam allowance all the way around. Using a knotted thread, sew a running stitch around the circle in the seam allowance. Leave a 1" thread tail. Place your fabric circle right side down on your pressing surface. Place the plastic washer in the center of the fabric, and pull on the thread tail. The seam will gather around the washer. While holding

the thread across the circle tightly, iron the fabric circle. Spray some Magic® Sizing or starch into the lid and use a cotton swab to paint the liquid onto the seam allowance of the circle. Iron again until dry, or mostly dry. I found that if I made four at a time, by the time I made the fourth one, the first one was dry.

When the circle is dry, loosen the gathering thread enough to pull out the plastic washer. After you remove the washer, gently pull on the thread tail to re-form the circle. Iron again. You now have a perfect circle with edges turned under, ready to appliqué!

I usually think about quilting designs while I'm making a quilt. To audition designs, I print out a line drawing of the quilt and start drawing possible quilting lines (fig. 6). This helps to eliminate ripping out when you don't like how a design looks, but I still had to do some ripping when my quilting doesn't turn out like I expect it to!

When deciding on quilting designs, I try to keep some unity between the various areas of the quilt. If I use a design in one area, I try to repeat the same design, or a variation, somewhere else. Many times I'll use the fabric as an inspiration. The bright red fabric in the very center of the star gave me the idea for all the scrolls.

Fig. 5.

Fig. 6.

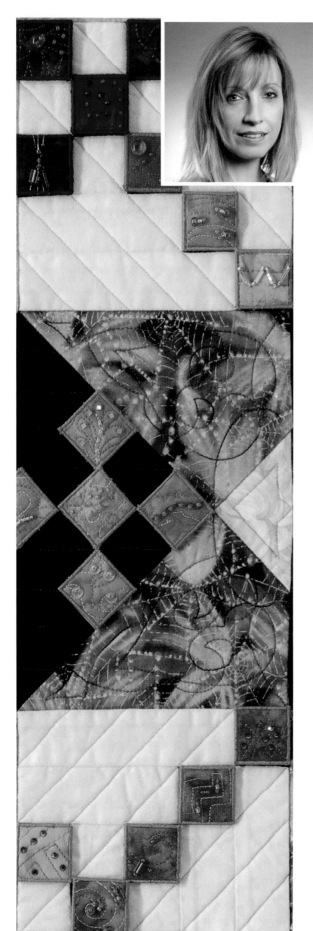

Fourth Place
Nadine Ruggles
Angelbachtal, Germany

Meet the Quilter

When I was a child, I created all sorts of arts and crafts in many different mediums. I made things I liked, in colors that I liked, whether it all belonged together or not. I made things for the sake of making them and it didn't matter much if they turned out perfect. I gave them to my parents or grandparents, and though it was great to see a smile of appreciation in response, it wasn't necessarily the reason that I created art.

But somewhere along the way, I began to believe that what others thought about my art was important. I began to depend on feedback from others, not just on the finished product, but concerning smaller design or color decisions during the creation process. When I lived closer to my mother, more often than not I'd ask her advice about colors, how this or that went together, what fabric to put with all of the others. As a new quilter, I depended on books to learn what was good and right about quilting and techniques, and I wanted to make my quilts look "right."

After I moved to Germany, I discovered (or maybe rediscovered) my own color sense and came to rely on myself more than others for these types of decisions. I found that I really could put colors together all by myself and be happy with the results. However, I spent a lot of time making sure my quilts were "right." I took classes from and studied books by well-known quilters, mastered the techniques, and used them in my own work, but never truly owned the methods. I looked at my quilts and saw echoes of other quilters there, instead of a work of art that was wholly my own. I was still working to please others, the viewers and the judges, instead of just working to please me.

When I look back at the quilts I've made, I see that the best ones are those that are completely my own—my own design; my color and fabric choices; my own challenges, mistakes, and solutions along the way. These quilts have helped me learn to create again and taught me to rely on my own artistic abilities. I've taken the

ELEMENTAL CHANGES: COLOR PLAY 60" x 60"

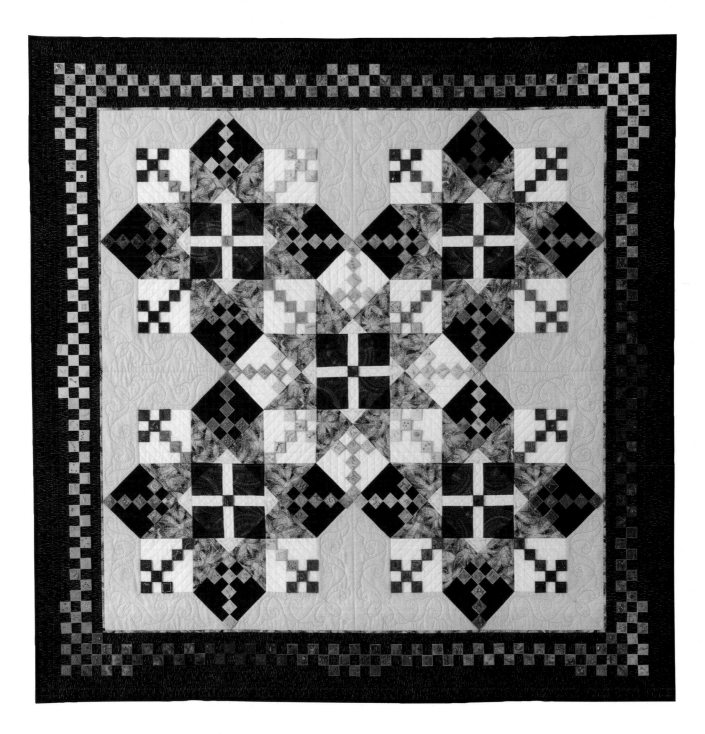

*"Playing with color is one of the most
exciting things about quilting for me."*

techniques I've learned from others and integrated them into my own workflow, done something different with them to create something totally new, and finally made them my own.

There are days when I have doubts about a design or a fabric, and wonder if it's "right," but then I remind myself that if I think it's good, then it is good, because I'm quilting for me. Though we are always learning from our own experiences and from other artists and quilters, we need to ask ourselves, "Who am I quilting for?" If you make a quilt and put it away, and no one ever sees it or admires it, is it worth making? It is, if you are quilting for you.

Inspiration and Design
Inchies Move In

Challenges like the New Quilts from an Old Favorite contest always appeal to me and though I may not enter a quilt every year, I always play around with the theme block to see if I can come up with a design that's worth putting into fabric. For Burgoyne Surrounded, I thought I'd like to design a quilt that would contain elements that could be moved around on the surface of the quilt. I worked with a few preliminary sketches and ideas and thought about how to temporarily attach the movable elements to the quilt. Would Velcro® tape work, or maybe magnets? What parts of the block would be movable? How big would the movable parts be?

During a break from designing, I decided to try making some Inchies for something different and fun. Inchies are 1" x 1" squares of embellished paper or fabric art. I found a tutorial on the Internet and gave them a try. I was instantly addicted to these diminutive works of art and realized that Inchies would be the perfect movable elements for the Burgoyne Surrounded quilt, since the original block contained many small squares. I could make a quilt with Inchies in all different colors that would be attached with Velcro and could be rearranged for a color play quilt (see photo, page 26).

The Inchies would be embellished with beads, fibers, wire, found objects, or anything else that could be sewn or glued on. They would add intricate detail and textural interest to the quilt. The Inchies would draw the viewer in for a closer look; after the first glance, it would be obvious that the Inchies were something more than just patchwork squares.

I chose my favorite of the Burgoyne Surrounded variation (fig. 1) and imported the block to Adobe® Photoshop® software.

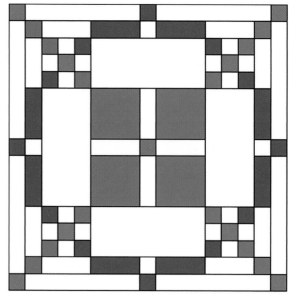

Fig. 1.

I pasted another copy of the drawing into a new layer in the same document, and set the blending mode to Multiply so I'd be able to see both layers. I removed the color from the top layer and rotated it by 45 degrees (fig. 2).

Fig. 2.

I could see a lovely eight-pointed star forming, so I erased some of the lines to simplify the block (fig. 3).

Fig. 3.

The center of the block could be further simplified for easier piecing and to highlight the four large center squares. Some quick calculations showed that if the small squares were just 1" x 1", the quilt wouldn't be very big with just one block, so I decided to center four more stars on the first, which meant that if each small square was to have an Inchie attached, I needed to make over 250 Inchies.

But the hazy plan in my head called for a quilt that actually had two sets of Inchies that could be swapped completely or rearranged in other ways. I decided to make one set in cool colors and one in warm colors for a total of over 500 unique Inchies! It seemed a daunting number and for a while the quilt was nicknamed "Epic Insanity." But the Inchies proved to be so addicting that it was a completely enjoyable process right down to the last one.

Technique
Coloring Your World

Playing with color is one of the most exciting things about quilting for me. I have a really difficult time limiting colors in my quilts and I have a "more is better" attitude about it most of the time. I believe you can use any colors together in a quilt and have success as long as the colors are smoothly blended together.

With my somewhat hazy plan in place, I purchased eight different assortments of batik fabric squares. I spent a happy hour or so culling and arranging 160 pieces into this palette of 128 blended fabrics (fig. 4), from each of which I would make four Inchies.

Fig, 4.

So how do you take 128 mixed colors and smoothly blend them together? When I choose and blend colors for a quilt, I use a something-on-its-way-to-something-else technique.

Take green and brown for instance. Look for fabrics that are green on-their-way-to-brown to place in between the two, to get from one color to the other. Think of a rainbow; you can't tell where one color stops and the next begins, but somehow, you get all the colors. When you are blending colors for a quilt in this manner, it's a spontaneous thing, and a variety of colors and values just happens naturally.

Practice this color technique by just playing with your stash of fabrics. Pick two seemingly unrelated colors, or two colors you think would never look good together in a quilt, and blend, experiment, and play. It is a learning process and with practice you'll be able to distinguish the most subtle differences in hue and value. You may be surprised by how easy it is to develop your own color sense and style.

I used this same technique to arrange the hundreds of Inchies on ELEMENTAL CHANGES: COLOR PLAY after the background quilt was complete. They are all attached with Velcro so they can be arranged and rearranged in infinite displays of beautifully blended color.

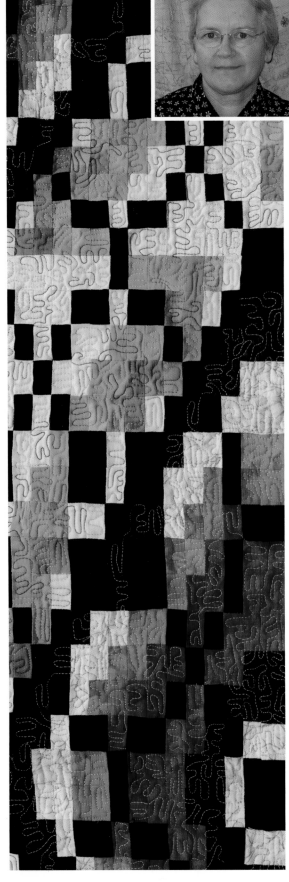

Fifth Place
Julia Graber
Brooksville, Mississippi

Meet the Quilter

Quilting has been a part of my life for many years. I grew up sewing my own clothes and making a few comforters and utility type quilts. Now in recent years I'm enjoying more of the contemporary and art quilts.

My parents owned a small fabric shop in Dayton, Virginia, where I worked briefly as a cashier. I remember fondling the fabric and dreaming of coordinating colors to make a top. They also made it possible for me to have a good sewing machine with upgrades most every year.

Two of my earlier quilts were made from my old dress fabric scraps for our children's bunk beds. I decided to use the Log Cabin block making half of the block with light scraps and half of it with dark scraps. Then I decided that instead of cutting strips for the logs, I would cut each log into small squares.

So, I did. That was the wrong thing for me to do at that stage of my quilting life, but I persevered and finished both tops. I had quilting bees and eventually finished up both quilts. They have served our family well for many years.

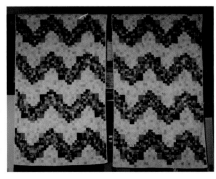

Today I enjoy piecing and designing bed quilts, wallhangings, art quilts, and postcards. I have taught a few classes here in our home and given a few lectures here and there. If you get a chance you may want to visit my Xanga site www.xanga.com/pauljuliagraber.

I consider myself to be a self-taught quilter, gleaning inspiration and receiving encouragement from a large family of quilters.

BUBBLED BURGOYNE 74½" x 74½"

*"I consider myself to be a self-taught quilter, gleaning inspiration
and receiving encouragement from a large family of quilters."*

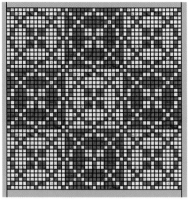

Fig. 1.

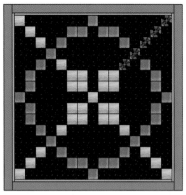

Fig. 2.

Fig. 3.

Fig. 4.

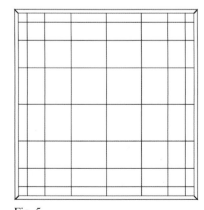

Fig. 5.

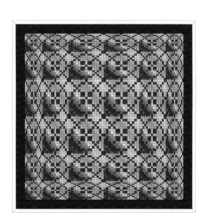

Fig. 6.

I've also learned a lot from reading magazines and books. In more recent years, I've taken a few workshops and classes that have complemented my knowledge of quilting.

Inspiration and Design

I am challenged by taking a traditional quilt block and transforming it into a more contemporary quilt; consequentially, the New Quilts from an Old Favorite contest has become a favorite of mine. The Burgoyne Surrounded quilt block commemorates the Revolutionary War Battle of Saratoga where British General John Burgoyne and his men were surrounded by American troops, causing Burgoyne's surrender in defeat on October 17, 1777. The traditional block usually has a white background with red squares and rectangles to form an X and O on the block. I used a solid black fabric for the Xs and Os and then chose red, green, and yellow for the background.

I used EQ6 to play with the block in different layouts and colors (figs. 1–4).

Trying an irregular grid (fig. 5) led to these layouts (figs. 6–9).

Here is the block that I used for my quilt (fig. 10, page 33).

Techniques

In studying my final layout, I decided I needed four identical blocks of each size. I cut strips of fabric, arranged them according to the row of the block that I was working on, and sewed them together. I did this for each row in the block (fig. 11).

Then I cut four strips from each fabric set and sewed them back together to get four blocks. I continued cutting and sewing strip-sets of different lengths and widths for each of the nine different sizes (some blocks are reversed). Then it was the simple task of sewing the 36 blocks together.

One challenge I faced was not taking a correct ¼" seam allowance on my first four center blocks. This made those blocks just a tad smaller, so I had to stretch and ease the blocks sewed next to them. I should have known better! Another challenge I faced was trying to get all the seams ironed in a correct direction so they would all nest together.

I made the thin inside trim by cutting a strip of the chartreuse fabric ¾" wide on the length of the grain. I sewed it to the edge of the quilts. Then I folded it over toward the edge (fig. 12) and ironed it down. After that I sewed on the double-folded bias binding as usual.

Fig. 7.

Fig. 8.

Fig. 9.

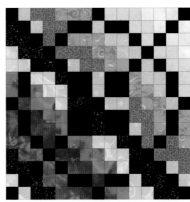

Fig. 10.

Fig. 11.

Fig. 12.

Finalist

Mae Adkins

Rawson, Ohio

Meet the Quilter

I've always been interested in quilting. As a small child my grandmother Mae Strode would let us cut out blocks and sew them together for the many quilts she made for the family through the years. Grandma would either tie or hand quilt them. I remember the hours we traced around a cardboard template and cut out with scissors. Most of her quilts were Nine-Patch style and it seemed like we were cutting forever for just one quilt. Early quilters had to have the patience of a saint.

My husband brought home my first cutting mat about 20 years ago. It was 3' x 5'. I spent many hours on my hands and knees on the floor learning how to use it. Quilting became much easier and more fun from that point on. I still have my mat but smaller mats for the table are a lot easier on the body. I would try a new pattern whenever I got a chance. At that time I hand quilted all my tops. I inherited my grandmother's quilt frame, which finally fell apart. I've had arthritis in my hands since I was twenty years old and no matter how hard I tried I could never get my stitches small or even enough.

Five years ago my sister Carol Shortsleeve invited me to go with her and some friends to the AQS Show in Paducah. After three days of viewing quilts and vendors I was really hooked. That was the first time I had even heard of machine quilting. I was amazed at how far quilting had progressed. I dreamed of owning a longarm quilting machine.

I found a longarm quilter in our area and sent my next three quilts to her. The only problem was that it just didn't seem like my work when I finally got the binding on. Part of the quilting experience just wasn't there. Nolting came out with an affordable longarm, the Hobby Quilter, an unregulated machine that would quilt a 12" area. I completed several quilts that year. I finally traded my Hobby Quilter in for the stitch-regulated Fun Quilter and Nolting designed a heavy duty frame to fit the machine. I can't imagine quilting without it.

THIRTEEN COLONIES—
STARS OF THE REVOLUTION 60½" x 79"

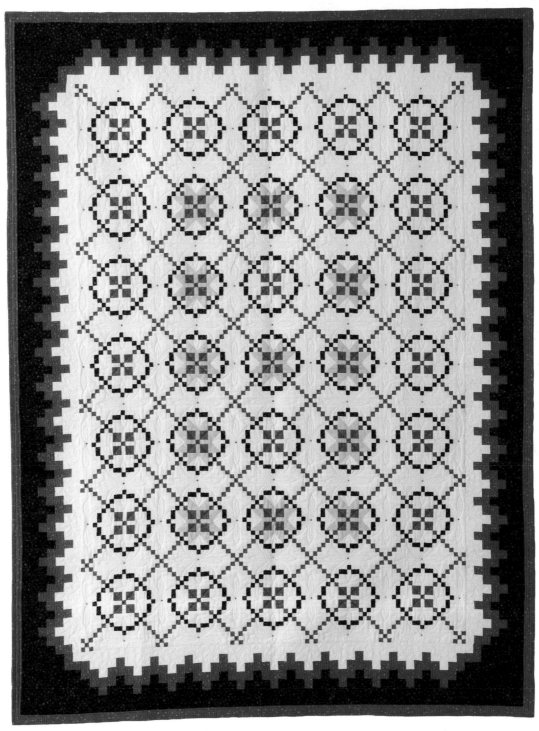

"I must give credit to my incredible husband, Doug. He spends his weekends quilt show hopping with me and no quilt shop is too far away."

Sharon Schamber has probably had the most influence on my quilting. Her work is so beautiful and inspires me to do better in all the details of quilting. I tried her method of foundation glue basting appliqué and machine stitching on the pieces. I can now start a piece and look forward to the finish. By watching her many videos I have learned how to free motion the quilts with some luck at success. I find that now I look at quilt patterns for what quilting possibilities they present.

My best suggestion to quilters is enter your quilts in area judged quilt shows or fairs. I have improved my quilting by using the judges' comments as a guide for what I need to do or learn about my quilting. Just keep in mind that each place you enter your quilts the judges see them differently and the competition is different. My PIECES OF BALTIMORE quilt won a first at a county fair, a first at state fair, but only third at a quilt show in Indiana last year.

Special thanks to my sister Carol (quilter and avid fan of Eleanor Burns) for the loan of her *Burgoyne Surrounded Quilt* book, which is out of print. In all my quilting I must give credit to my incredible husband, Doug. He spends his weekends quilt show hopping with me and no quilt shop or show is too far away. He took his vacation for a road trip to Paducah in order to obtain a contest entry form.

I met a lady at our annual quilt show in Bluffton last year and she said that at one time she was as passionate about quilting as I am. She told me, "But as I am 80, I've finally tapered off." There is hope for my husband if he doesn't starve to death first!

Design and Inspiration

Quilt teacher, judge, and good friend Betty Fiser's belief in me inspired my involvement in this year's competition. After watching the *Quilt in a Day* video on the Burgoyne Surrounded history, it seemed amazing that thirteen small colonies could win a war against the well-trained British and French soldiers.

The rectangles around the center Nine-Patch seemed like the perfect place to put corner square triangles to form the stars. The original block was too large for thirteen blocks, so I divided the measurements in half to get the desired layout with the Star block surrounded by plain blocks (fig. 1).

Fig. 1.

The next step was deciding on the color and fabrics. Red, white, and blue seemed like the only natural colors to represent our country. At our local quilt shop I found star fabric in these colors, although I changed the white for a cream-on-cream background. I've found in my experience most white fabrics aren't dense enough without putting a lining fabric behind them. Bright yellow fabric completed the choices for the top. In the first block I made, I used the cream-on-cream fabric in the center nine-patch, but it just didn't stand out. I remade the block replacing the cream-on-cream with yellow and it really stood out around General Burgoyne. I strip-pieced all the nine-patch sections.

Assembling the quilt was another challenge. All the 1" finished square strip-sets had to be pieced together. I decided to use Elmer's® Washable School Glue in the seam allowance. Glue basting is much more precise than pinning to keep the seams from shifting. It took about a week to finish the blocks and sashings.

The next hurdle was the border. I'm a quilter who thinks the more borders the better. I think borders really make a quilt stand out. My favorite form of quilting is appliqué but I just couldn't come up with a design that didn't take away from the stars. After about a month with the pieced top hanging on my design board with no inspiration, I was looking through *Foundation Borders* by Jane Hall and Dixie Haywood for a border idea to finish another quilt I was working on. When I saw Dixie's Bargello Borders it seemed like the perfect solution to the multiple border I wanted.

Remember the old computer paper that came in folder perforated sheets? I knew I kept it all these years for a reason. I drew out my quilt measurements on the paper and adjusted the design to fit the quilt. I then strip-pieced the border. I was really delighted with the results.

This quilt was only the second quilt I ever used free-motion machine quilting on. I knew I wanted to change colors of thread to match the quilt top. Betty told me several years ago that the backing should be a busy print with the color that I intended to use in my thread. After a road trip to several quilt shops in Michigan, I finally found the flag background with an old world look. They had just enough to fit the top.

I used a heavyweight poly batting to ensure the backing wouldn't shadow through the top. I find it's a good weight for quilts that will be hanging on a wall. If I'd had more experience at the time I would have quilted fireworks in the cream background, but every sample I tried just didn't look right. After quilting and binding, I added red and white crystals for glitz (fig. 2).

Fig. 2.

Finalist
Jean Biddick
Tucson, Arizona

Meet the Quilter

Sewing has always been part of my life and I can't remember when I learned to sew. When I was very small my hand embroidery projects were kept in the bottom drawer of my mother's tall sewing cabinet. It was the only drawer I could reach. I don't remember learning to use the sewing machine but know it was long before my feet could touch the ground. The sewing machine was operated by a knee lever instead of a foot pedal, so being able to reach the ground was not an issue.

Although my mother did not make quilts, she did sew nearly everything else and there was always a box of scraps in the closet. Those are the scraps I used for my first quilt project. It was a crazy quilt that I started when I was in junior high school and it is still unfinished. By the time I was in the all-my-friends-are-having-babies phase of my life I had amassed a scrap box of my own. I cut squares from those fabrics and made simple tied baby quilts as gifts. After making a few dozen of those basic quilts I was given a book about machine piecing and I was off on an amazing journey.

I love complex geometric designs and enjoy figuring out how to interpret those intricate designs as pieced quilts. Machine piecing has become my specialty. The feeling of accomplishment when the pieces fit perfectly is a real joy. As much as I like the process of quilting, my real love is teaching. Sharing what I know about machine piecing and watching students improve their skills is very satisfying. I love meeting a former student and hearing, "Every time I pin a point I hear your voice in my head" or "When I came to a hard intersection I asked myself, how would Jean do this?"

I am thrilled to be able to give students the technical skills they need to be able to turn their own quilting ideas into completed quilts. After 25 years of teaching machine-piecing techniques I still find myself learning from my students. The give and take

SARATOGA SUNSHINE 58" x 58"

"Machine piecing has become my speciality. The feeling of accomplishment when the pieces fit perfectly is a real joy."

Fig. 1.

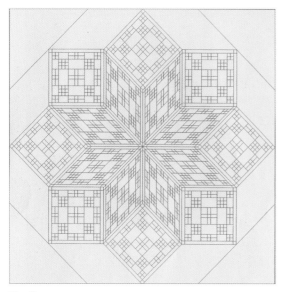

Fig. 2.

Fig. 3.

and sharing that has always been part of quiltmaking is something very special. The friends I have made along my quiltmaking journey are truly the best part of being a quilter.

Inspiration and Design

When I first saw that Burgoyne Surrounded was the block chosen for this year's New Quilts from an Old Favorite contest, I knew this was the year I would finally enter the competition. I've looked at this block many times over the years and have always wanted to use it for a quilt. The added incentive to use it in a different way was just what I needed to get going. I love that the block is made up of only squares and rectangles yet offers lots of room for interpretation. There are so many ways to color the basic block to emphasize different aspects of the design that I knew I'd enjoy playing with it.

I used EQ6 from the Electric Quilt Company to work on my design. I wanted to see what would happen if I skewed the Burgoyne block into different shapes. EQ6 allows you to start with a block outline and place other pieced blocks into each of the sections of the original block. I started with a Lemoyne Star block and placed a Burgoyne block into each diamond, square, and setting triangle of that star design (fig. 1). I had great fun playing with colorings of my design, but was not entirely satisfied with any of them. I decided to try again with a different 8-pointed star for my layout and reworked the design using a Rolling Star block as my base. The new design (fig. 2) felt much more finished with square versions of the Burgoyne block surrounding the central star. The new design included lots of empty space in the corners and I needed to design borders to fill those large empty corners.

With the Rolling Star design extending into the border areas I was having trouble figuring out how to draw my borders in EQ6. I know there is a way to do that, but I was too anxious to finish my design to take the time to learn how to do it. My solution was to draw the border ideas separately from the completed Rolling Star design (figs. 3 & 4). I cut out my colored version of the Rolling Star and placed it over several different print-outs of possible border designs until I found the right combination. I settled on an inner border of squares and rectangles and an outer border of pieced checkmarks.

Originally I colored the pieced borders with two values of turquoise on an orange background (as shown in fig. 3). I pieced one corner of the border section and added it to the pieced star. Disaster! The turquoise took over and made the star look dull. I'm so glad I had only made and attached one of the corners. I went back to the design software and tried out other colorings. The rusty red and brown fabrics worked much better (fig. 5).

The quilting designs underwent changes as well. Most sections of the quilt were quilted at least twice and some were quilted three times. Designs that I thought would enhance the piecing simply did not do their job. I think I spent at least as much time removing quilting stitches as I did putting quilting stitches in! I know there are quilters who design an entire quilt and sew it exactly as it was designed. I am not one of those quilters. I always have to see what it actually looks like in fabric and I always give myself permission to change my mind along the way. I have to listen to the voice in my head that says, "That's not right, try something else." It often means more work, but it also makes a better quilt.

Technique

My approach to machine piecing is pretty basic. Pieces are rotary cut with the seam allowance included. I use templates, again with the seam allowance included, for any odd-shaped pieces. Although paper piecing can help with accuracy it is not my method of choice. I find it more difficult to control the grainline and the direction in which the seam allowances are pressed with paper piecing than with a more traditional approach. I am also not a fan of the "cut the pieces a little bit too big and true them up later" approach. That just adds an extra step to the whole process. Good basic piecing skills that I can rely on for perfect points and consistent accuracy have served me well.

The outer pieced border looks complicated, but is actually quite easy to make. I designed it years ago in a Peaky and Spike class with Doreen Speckmann. This is the second time I've used this border treatment.

The interlocking checkmark design is a series of pieced squares that alternate in their coloring. The square is divided into two triangles and each of the triangles is further divided with simple straight lines drawn from the corner or midpoint of the square (fig. 6). The corner block is drawn by connecting the midpoints of two adjacent sides of the square (fig. 7).

Fig. 4.

Fig. 5

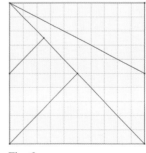

Fig. 6.

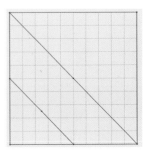

Fig. 7.

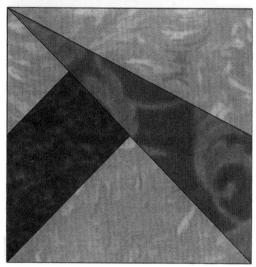

Fig. 8.

My border uses a 2½" square, but the design can be made in any size. There are two colorings of the block (fig. 8) in the border and when alternated these two squares create the interlocking checkmarks (fig. 9). Use a mirror image of the block if you want the checkmarks to change direction in the center of the border (fig. 10).

One half of the basic block is fairly easy to sew. It has nice square corners that make it easy to align the pieces (fig. 11, page 43). The half with the two long skinny triangles is a bit more challenging.

Draw the templates on graph paper and add the seam allowances. Add a line at the long narrow point perpendicular to the edge that will be sewn between the two triangles and ¼" past the point of the actual patch (indicated by the circle in fig. 12). Trim the tails along that line.

Join the two pieced triangles to complete the square unit. Pressing the seam toward the three-section unit will allow you to mesh the seams as you join two squares and build the border row. Pressing the seam between the two triangle units open will reduce some of the bulk. Neither choice is perfect, but either of them works well.

Planning ahead is always a good idea. Knowing how one choice will affect the next step of the piecing process will help ensure that things fit together well. Thinking ahead helps to avoid unwelcome surprises later in the piecing process.

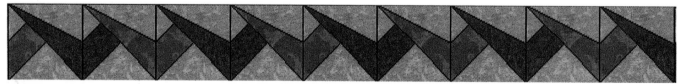

Fig. 9.

Fig. 10.

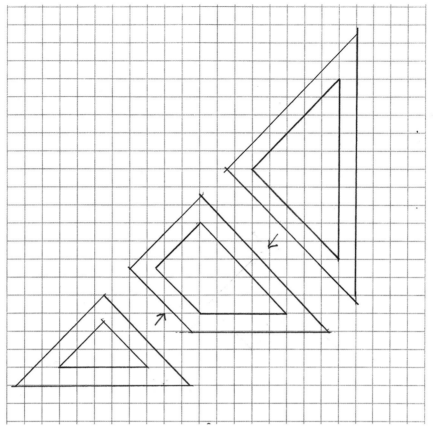

Fig. 11.

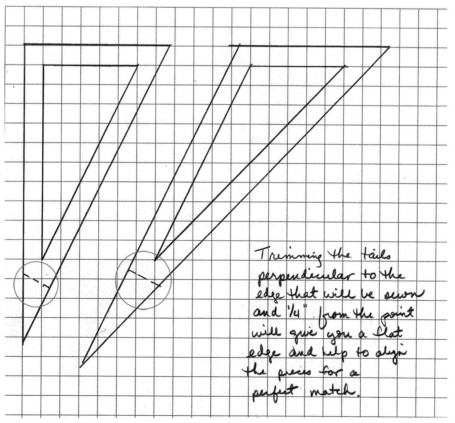

Trimming the tails perpendicular to the edge that will be sewn and ¼" from the point will give you a flat edge and help to align the pieces for a perfect match.

Fig. 12.

Photo by Eric Davis

Mary Kay Davis

Sunnyvale, California

Meet the Quilter

I began sewing to make clothes for my dolls. My early efforts were scraps sewn with a needle and thread, but they were ball gowns to me. In junior high I had the requisite home economics class where I made my first quilt. It was typical of the time and made up of scraps from my clothes. I don't think it was truly meant to be raw-edge appliqué, but it works for me. It has puffy batting and is tied. The binding is hemstitched on the back.

Sewing gave me an early career as I did piecework for my brother's waterbed company. I would sew upholstery pieces on my mother's Elna. (I'm sure she was thrilled.) By the time I was a teenager, my mom paid for me to have sewing lessons. She herself was an excellent seamstress, but did it out of necessity and found no real joy in it. Once I was able to sew, she had me sew for her instead.

While I sewed clothes through high school and college, including my wedding gown, I never made another quilt until I stepped into my local quilt shop, The Granary, in Sunnyvale, California, around 1996. (By the way, I believe the Granary is one of the oldest quilt shops in America.) I signed up for a Quilt-as-You-Go class. It was great. The instructor taught hand and machine piecing. I learned how to use templates and to hand appliqué. I also thought you had to complete the quilt by the time class was finished, in four weeks. That was the first and last quilt that I ever hand quilted.

I enjoyed the class but wasn't really bit by the quilting bug. I'm not entirely sure when that happened, possibly when I got a new sewing machine around 1999 for my 10th wedding anniversary. (It was a good anniversary; my husband gave me a new sewing machine and a diamond ring. My 20th anniversary is in April 2009 and I'm really looking forward to it!) It was around this time that my mom became ill and I ended up leaving my "real" job to be with my dad. I had much more time on my hands and I think that's when quilting began to take up some of that time.

SHIMMERING SIGHT 54" x 54"

"Around 2004, I entered my first major quilt challenge and took first place. From then on, I was hooked on challenges."

Small Flying Geese Unit

Use Paper Piece Pattern #2 (page 49).

Cut 1 aqua rectangle 2¼" by 1⅝" and 2 white rectangles 2¼" x 1½". Use your favorite paper-piecing method to construct the block. Trim. Press to the white. You'll need 8 units per block.

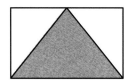

Skinny Flying Geese Unit

Use Paper Piece Pattern #3 (page 49).

Cut 1 black rectangle 6½" x 1⅝" and 2 blue rectangles 1¾" x 4". Use your favorite paper-piecing method to construct the block. Trim. Press to the blue. You'll need 4 units per block.

Four-Patch

All the squares are cut 1" x 1". You'll need 2 blue and 2 white squares per unit. Assemble as shown below. Press toward the blue. If you are making more than one block, these could be strip-pieced. You'll need 8 units per block.

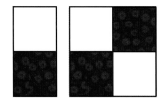

Half-Square Triangles

Cut 1 black 2" x 2" square and 1 blue 2" x 2" square. Place the blue square on top of the black square, right sides together. Mark one square from corner to corner, as shown in red. Stitch ¼" from both sides of red line. Cut along red line. Open and press toward black. This will create two half-square triangle units. Trim squares to 1⁹⁄₁₆" x 1⁹⁄₁₆". You will need 8 units per block.

Assemble the Burgoyne Surrounded Block

Assemble the block in rows.

Then add the sashing.

The altered Burgoyne Surrounded block.

SHIMMERING SIGHT 54" x 54"

"Around 2004, I entered my first major quilt challenge and took first place. From then on, I was hooked on challenges."

I attended a couple of quilt camps and made quilting friends. I joined a small quilt group. I eventually joined our guild, the Santa Clara Valley Quilt Association. This guild founded the San Jose Museum of Quilts and Textiles and is very active in the community.

Around 2004, I entered my first major quilt challenge and took first place. From then on, I was hooked on challenges. Challenges have really expanded my quilting horizon because they always have a deadline, and they usually make me go outside the box. They have even given me the chance to travel to places like Paducah to see my quilts (although my quilts travel more than I do).

My biggest thrill came when I entered the P&B Textiles Morning Garden Challenge. The challenge was to use Alex Anderson's Morning Garden fabric line to create the quilt. I was at the Granary when I got the call from P&B that I had won. Not only would I receive a prize, but the shop would get a visit from Alex herself. I burst into tears and so did the owner of the shop.

Since that time I've continued to work at the Granary. I started a small pattern company, Threads on the Floor, which I currently sell only at the Granary and on my Web site, www.mkdthreads.com. Quilting has taken over a huge part of my life, particularly as my children get older. It allows me to be creative and lowers my blood pressure at the same time.

Inspiration and Design

I made my first trip to Paducah last year to visit a quilt I had hanging in the museum as part of the Quilts from the Pacific Rim exhibit. Also hanging at the time was the New Quilts from an Old Favorite exhibit that featured the Sawtooth pattern. I thought the quilts were wonderful and decided I wanted to enter the next year's contest. I admit to being a little bit stumped by Burgoyne Surrounded. I had to research the block to find out its history, but I still had never really seen many quilts that used the block. I decided to forge ahead.

I wanted to make the quilt very patriotic and factor in the whole Revolutionary War theme. I had just found

out that I could qualify as a Daughter of the American Revolution. So, I think I was attuned to the birth of our nation. I also wanted to make the whole quilt be one large Burgoyne Surrounded block. I was going to use the empty spaces for appliqué or quilting. I had grandiose ideas for eagles and drums, possibly an army marching around the border. I started to put it together but decided that it was going to end up being too traditional. Besides, appliqué is not my strong point. I have a hard time wasting effort and fabric, so I completed AMERICAN ALL-STAR (fig. 1) as my 9/11 quilt for the year. I do a patriotic quilt every year around that time as a remembrance.

Fig. 1. AMERICAN ALL-STAR

For my next attempt, I decided I wanted to keep the Burgoyne block intact, but add to it. I also wanted to change the color palette. Blue and green are my favorite colors so I was able to create the entire quilt from my stash. I then decided to make smaller blocks. They are 10" x 10" finished. If you look at the quilt, you'll see that the Burgoyne block is there in its entirety with just the addition of a few triangles. Each block has over 150 pieces, some of which are pretty tiny. I had to be patient and organized about putting everything together. I went from a single block quilt to one with over 3000 pieces. Sometimes, you just don't want to count.

I felt strongly about the quilt having movement. I was hoping to achieve the effect of looking at a mirage, where the air seems to shimmer in waves. I attempted to create the movement by changing the background colors and setting triangles, as the blocks themselves are very busy. Adding black and white to the quilt seemed to jazz it up, so I tossed them into the mix. SHIMMERING SIGHT doesn't really give your eyes a place to rest and this contributes to its movement.

I added the New York Beauty blocks as my good luck charm, again, to create movement, and added the checkerboard border. This border is always one of my favorites and keeps your eye traveling around the quilt.

Originally, this quilt was going to be titled BURGOYNE SURROUNDED BY THE BEAUTY OF NEW YORK. My family thought that was too much of a mouthful and didn't really understand the history behind the name. So it was dubbed SHIMMERING SIGHT as a reflection of my feelings about movement and mirages.

Technique

SHIMMERING SIGHT is made up of only two different blocks, the altered Burgoyne Surrounded and the New York Beauty block. The sashing is actually part of the altered Burgoyne block. I used Electric Quilt 6 to create the foundations for the parts I needed to paper piece. I was able to piece the rest of the block normally. These are the instructions for the 10" Burgoyne Surrounded block.

Center Nine-Patch

The four green corner squares are cut at 1⁹⁄₁₆" x 1⁹⁄₁₆". The white strips are cut at 1" x 1⁹⁄₁₆". The green center square is cut 1" x 1". Assemble as shown below. Press to green. If you are making more than one block, these could be strip-pieced. You'll need 1 unit per block.

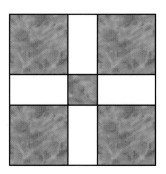

Side Six-Patch

The white and green rectangles are cut at 1⁹⁄₁₆" by 1". The white and green squares are cut at 1" x 1". Assemble as shown. Press to green. These could also be strip-pieced. You'll need 4 units per block.

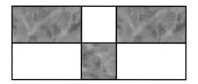

Large Flying Geese Unit

Use Paper Piece Pattern #1 (page 49).
Cut one aqua rectangle 2½" x 3½" for the center of the Flying Geese unit.

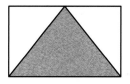

Cut 2 white 2¼" x 3¾" rectangles for the sides. These rectangles could even be cut a bit larger. I always want to make sure there is enough fabric when I'm paper-piecing at an angle. Use your favorite paper-piecing method to construct the unit. Trim. Press to the white. You'll need 4 units per block.

Nine-Patch

All the squares are cut 1" x 1". You'll need two blue, three green, and four white squares per unit.

Assemble as shown below. Press toward the blue and green. If you are making more than one block, these could be strip-pieced. You'll need four units per block.

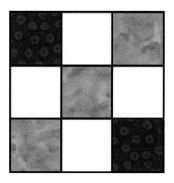

Small Flying Geese Unit

Use Paper Piece Pattern #2 (page 49).

Cut 1 aqua rectangle 2¼" by 1⅝" and 2 white rectangles 2¼" x 1½". Use your favorite paper-piecing method to construct the block. Trim. Press to the white. You'll need 8 units per block.

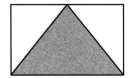

Skinny Flying Geese Unit

Use Paper Piece Pattern #3 (page 49).

Cut 1 black rectangle 6½" x 1⅝" and 2 blue rectangles 1¾" x 4". Use your favorite paper-piecing method to construct the block. Trim. Press to the blue. You'll need 4 units per block.

Four-Patch

All the squares are cut 1" x 1". You'll need 2 blue and 2 white squares per unit. Assemble as shown below. Press toward the blue. If you are making more than one block, these could be strip-pieced. You'll need 8 units per block.

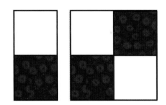

Half-Square Triangles

Cut 1 black 2" x 2" square and 1 blue 2" x 2" square. Place the blue square on top of the black square, right sides together. Mark one square from corner to corner, as shown in red. Stitch ¼" from both sides of red line. Cut along red line. Open and press toward black. This will create two half-square triangle units. Trim squares to 1⁹⁄₁₆" x 1⁹⁄₁₆". You will need 8 units per block.

Assemble the Burgoyne Surrounded Block

Assemble the block in rows.

Then add the sashing.

The altered Burgoyne Surrounded block.

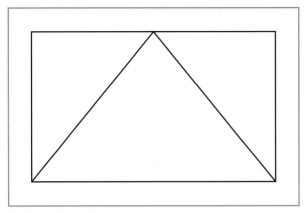

#1 Large Flying Geese

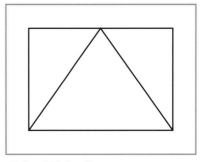

#2 Small Flying Geese

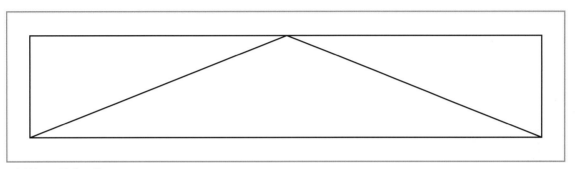

#3 Skinny Flying Geese

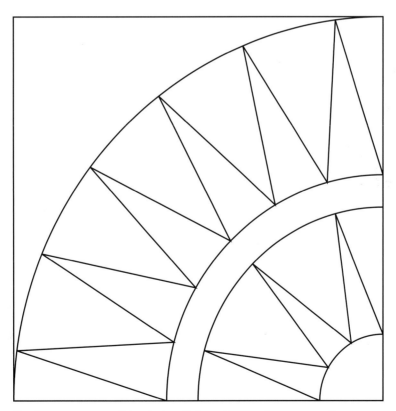

Border cornerstone quilting design. Enlarge 125% and use two motifs on corner setting triangles.

Photo by Bruce Kushnick

Finalist

Ann Feitelson

Montague, Massachusetts

Meet the Quilter

I grew up surrounded by pattern. My mother and I knitted avidly, did needlepoint, and sewed garments from wildly patterned cottons. She had fabulous taste in fabric, wallpaper, color, and clothing and transmitted those delights to me. She adored volunteering in the textile department of the Cooper Hewitt Museum in New York City. Although she didn't make quilts, she bought 1930s' quilts for me to sleep under.

She took me to see the ground-breaking 1971 exhibit at the Whitney Museum, Abstract Design in American Quilts. I loved those big, bold quilts. I undertook my first quilt shortly afterwards, just after graduating from college; it was based on a Flying Geese quilt in that exhibit. Of course these feminine interests in visually exciting textiles—knitting and quilting— were nothing you could study in college or graduate school at the time. I studied painting, earned a master's degree, and taught painting at the college level, continuing to knit and sew as hobbies.

I painted landscapes and still-lifes seriously—maybe too seriously. I stopped painting in 1983. Needing to diversify and expand my interests in art, I turned to writing about all aspects of the arts for local newspapers (I still write photography reviews) and completed a master's degree in art history. I wrote a book on knitting, *The Art of Fair Isle Knitting*, still in print after 13 years, and I have taught many knitting classes. I work part-time in a yarn store.

Fair Isle knitting is based on dual color sequences—a shaded pattern against a shaded background. This principle of organizing color, based on combining shaded color sequences, remains a habit in how I work with color.

I love color. It speaks to me of ecstasy and the sublime. It's like music, emotional and vibrant, located in an ideal world. Color

BATIKS BEGUILE BURGOYNE 68" x 68"

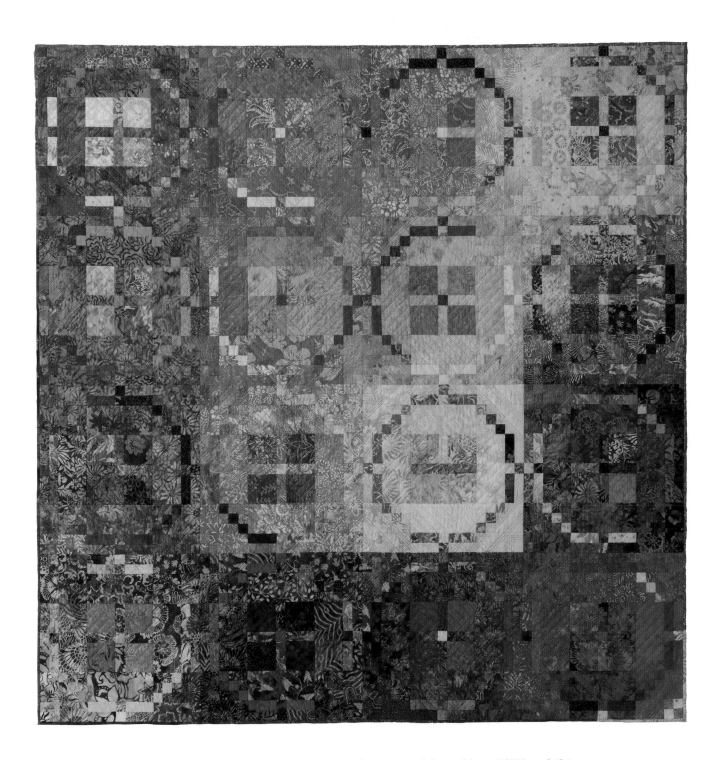

*"My mother took me to see the ground-breaking 1971 exhibit
at the Whitney Museum, Abstract Design in American Quilts.
I undertook my first quilt shortly afterwards."*

sequences always glow; using them seems to give color an almost magical power. I start with one sequence, then add other sequences that shift, reverse, or echo it, which adds to the luminous effect. Interrelationships in multiple contexts shimmer. I enjoy putting color though several systematic paces. But I also try to remain free with it; all that really matters is whether it looks good.

And I love batiks. Not only the tight weave and fine cloth, but the fluid, organic look of the designs, which come from the nature of the process, the molten wax and flowing dyes. The rivers of dyes, the irregularities of chance blots and splashes, harmonize with batiks' natural motifs of leaves, seeds, flowers, and feathers. Batiks often use analogous colors (orange and yellow, for example) so when the dyes intermix they don't become muddy (as red and green would). The analogous colors blend well into my even larger sequences.

For quite a while I subscribed to a fabric shipment of fat sixteenths of all the newest batiks that one shop received. I love having a wide variety of fabrics and an extensive color palette. I don't ever want a whole lot of any one fabric.

Inspiration & Design

An early trial block used essentially six fabrics (fig. 1). Even with that (to me) small number of fabrics, I sequenced them—light, medium, and dark purples for the background; a dark blue, medium blue-green, and light/bright blue multi-shading in the opposite direction, dark to light, for the motif. But I wanted even more visual activity and complexity. I wanted the batiks to really dance and sing and party.

I usually start with one or two big gradations as a compositional foundation. I arranged my fat sixteenths in a red-to-yellow sequence, which I spread out from the top left of the quilt. The four squares in the centers of the blocks in the top row use the same colors and the same fabrics as the backgrounds. but they shade in the opposite direction, yellows on the left to reds on the right. So there's a sequence and a mirror-image of it, crossing paths. When I began, I had not foreseen

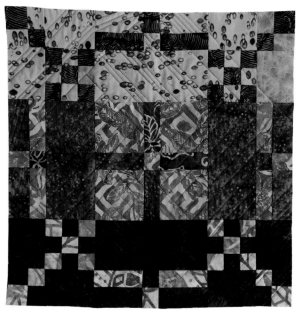

Fig. 1.

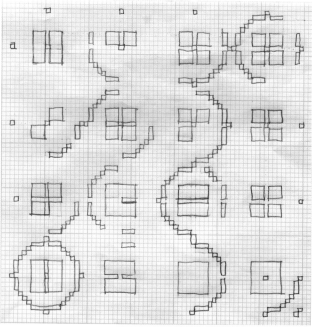

Fig. 2 .

how the four central squares would oppose the main drift of color.

You could call my process intuitive, but trial-and-error might be more accurate because I'm often displeased with my first ideas. I stumble uncertainly for a time, urging myself onward in spite of what seem like mistakes and wrong turns. I agonize. The creative process reminds me of E. L. Doctorow's description of writing a novel: it's like driving in the fog; you can't see where you're going. I started this quilt and abandoned it several times. Finally I found the commitment to see it through. I wound up needing much more contrast than I initially thought I would because of the high contrast within the batiks. I had to counterbalance the hot, bright colors somehow; the turquoise and purple had not been part of my original vision.

The Burgoyne Surrounded block is so square and made of so many squares (65 of them to be exact and 32 rectangles, at least in the variation of the block that I used) that the traditional block seems quite contained, even constrained. But I wanted the blocks and the quilt to seem open and expansive. The block hints at curves, as I discovered when I made an initial drawing (fig. 2).

It is symmetrical, but I wanted color to destabilize the blocks, blur boundaries, and describe arcs. I tried to see the block in radical ways, as far from its traditional four dark squares on a white background as possible. I made the values work both ways—light squares on dark and dark squares on light. I tried to reconfigure the block visually, joining some elements to make new shapes, like the large S-curves, or the short bars between the central squares, which make vertical or horizontal elements here and there (fig. 3). In the bottom right block, the four squares and the four bars become one large turquoise square (fig. 4).

Quilting a top is usually a linear and textural problem, but for me it becomes interesting when I can make it a color question as well. I change thread color frequently so that it either matches the surrounding areas, or opposes them.

Fig. 3.

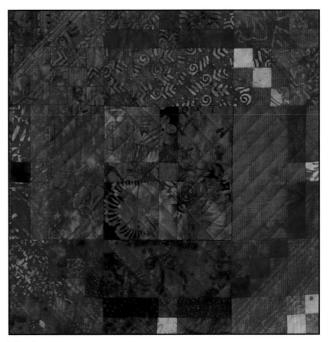

Fig. 4.

Photo by Michael Bersin

Finalist

Joan Ferguson

Warrensburg, Missouri

Meet the Quilter

In 1993 a friend asked me if I would like to attend a quilting workshop that was being offered at a local church. We would be making a star table runner. Out of curiosity I went and made my table runner in holiday colors. My mother puts it on her table every December—flat points and all. After this workshop I was so hooked on quilting! I continued to take classes until late 1995 and early 1996 when I started working more on my own. Up until this time I had been making all of my quilts in a class or workshop setting. In 1996 I entered a wallhanging in the Missouri State Fair and it won a blue ribbon, which stunned me. After that, everything started to snowball. I still take classes to learn as much as I can.

In my real life I am a musician. I play the harp professionally at weddings, corporate events, and with several symphonies in western Missouri, and I teach privately. In other words, I do not have a steady work schedule. With the current economic downturn, I am working less than I used to 8–10 years ago and this gives me lots of time to quilt—and go fabric shopping. I do not get a lot done with my quilting during times of the year when I am busier with music, but that gives the rest of the year to quilt and shop! April is a slow month, so I have plenty of time to attend the AQS show in Paducah, Kentucky!

I think what I enjoy most about quilting is the creative outlet it gives me when the music business slows down. While I enjoy reading and puttering in my weed garden, it is nice to create something beautiful. After attending several of the big national quilt shows and lots of state and local guild shows, I have come to believe that quilting is truly an art form, right up there with music.

I am often inspired by music when I contemplate my next quilt. Several of my quilts even have song titles: 'ROUND MIDNIGHT and YOU CAN CALL ME AL. The other thing that most inspires my quilting is nature. I used to live in Arizona and on the northern

54   BURGOYNE SURROUNDED: New Quilts from an Old Favorite

TURNING POINT 74½" x 74½"

"One of the most enduring musical forms is the theme and variations. Music and quilting have a lot in common."

coast of California and like to work the colors of the desert and ocean into my quilts. As far as the future goes, I plan to do more nature quilts such as close-up shots of a butterfly on a flower or a cactus flower in full bloom.

In addition to not having steady work hours, I also do not have children. I do, however, have a husband and Michael is one of my biggest cheerleaders. He is also a musician and has developed a very keen eye for quilts. He has traveled with me to Paducah and Nashville for past AQS shows when my quilts have hung there. When he goes fabric shopping with me (not all that often) he will even hold my purse for me. Most of all, he enjoys sleeping under my quilts because he knows of all the work and love I put into them.

Inspiration and Design

I have always been interested in the Revolutionary War era. Our eighth grade history teacher, Mr. Upton, taught the history of the war from the British standpoint, much to the chagrin of many of our parents. When I started quilting in 1993, I learned that there was a quilt block inspired by General John Burgoyne's surrender to Major General Horatio Gates at the second battle of Saratoga. Since then I have wanted to make a quilt using this block but somehow it was always pushed to the back burner by other quilt projects, work, and just plain life. When the museum announced that the New Quilts from an Old Favorite block for 2009 was Burgoyne Surrounded, I decided that this was the time to act. Although my finished quilt does not use the traditional block, it was fun researching and designing my variation.

To begin, I bought Eleanor Burns' *Burgoyne Surrounded Quilt* and Elizabeth Hamby Carlson's *Burgoyne Surrounded: A Classic Quilt Plus Six Variations*. I also decided to read a history of the Saratoga battles and bought *Saratoga: Turning Point of America's Revolutionary War* by Richard M. Ketchum. I carefully studied the Burns and Carlson books to get an idea of traditional block size, color, and quilting patterns. The variations presented in Carlson's book are beautiful, but I realized I wanted to do something a little more "out there" and off the beaten path.

As a musician I know that one of the most enduring musical forms is the theme and variations. Over the years I have performed many such pieces on the harp and have come to realize that music and quilting have a lot in common. In music when we vary a theme it is usually done in the melody, harmony, rhythm, meter, tempo, or dynamics. With a quilt it can involve the size, color, layout, or shape. Embellishments can be added; we can paint or use a release agent such as bleach to create different effects on the surface of our quilts. We can appliqué something that is traditionally pieced or piece something that is traditionally appliquéd.

From the start I knew I wanted to do something different with the color. It seemed the traditional Burgoyne Surrounded quilts were red and white, blue and white, or scrappy quilts. The two-color quilts are beautiful, but not very me. And my classically trained musician's brain has a hard time coming to grips with the concept of a scrappy quilt. Not enough order! Before I knew what colors I was going to use in this quilt I started adding fun, bright colors to my design and they started growing on me. I realized the square- and diamond-shaped chains were the perfect place to use some of the beautiful gradated fabrics available today.

In the end I think the thing I like best about this quilt is the way the colors sparkle. The lightest shades of green and orange really glow against the dark navy blue. I will probably try making this quilt again, although I think I will stagger the point where I start the graduated color in each row so all the darks and all the lights would not meet at the same place. That would probably give a more three-dimensional effect than it has now.

Technique

One of the biggest challenges in making this quilt was figuring out how to do something different with the setting. After several early bland and very square attempts, I decided to tweak the layout by checking out what the layout libraries had available in Electric Quilt 5. I noticed a section titled Special Effects. I investigated further and discovered a setting—Special Effects 9—that would vary the shape of the traditional square blocks to diamonds and triangles; four of the blocks were still square, but set on point. All of the triangle blocks are on the outside edge (figs. 1–2).

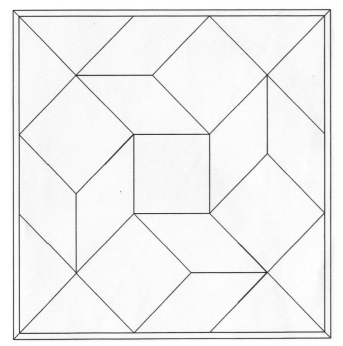

Fig. 1.

Fig. 2.

I decided to use New York Beauty in four of them. As I started adding color to the blocks, I realized I had finally found what I was looking for. I drafted the New York Beauty blocks after I completed the other blocks of the quilt so I could get an accurate size for the triangle, which I measured off the other four triangle blocks in the quilt.

Several years ago our local newspaper put an ad in the paper offering their roll ends of newsprint for 25 cents a pound. For one dollar you got a whole lot of paper to play with. This paper is 28" wide and is perfect for drawing larger quilt blocks. I realized my New York Beauty blocks would need to be drafted on this large paper and I drew out a triangle and went to work using some string and a couple of pencils as my large-scale compass.

After settling on a nice size arc, I took a ruler and started on the spikes. In the end I went with spikes that filled the area nicely—from the large center spike to the gradually smaller ones at the sides (fig. 3). I drew over the pencil lines with a permanent marker. Then I traced four copies of the spike section on newsprint to use as foundation patterns. I made templates of the arc section and the two upper parts of the block on either side of the spike section on freezer paper.

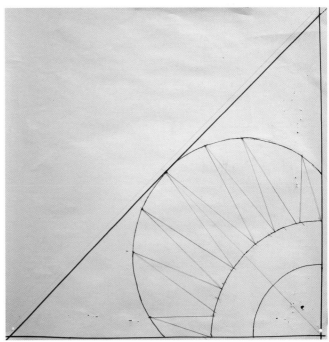

Fig. 3.

After taking the paper off the spike section, I pinned it to the arc, matching the center and the ends, pinning every ⅛"–¼", then I sewed the curves very slowly. This usually eliminates the need to rip and resew. I did the same with the two upper sections, using lots of pins and sewing slowly, and pressed the triangle block with the seam allowances towards the spikes.

Finalist
Sandi Fruehling
Aurora, Colorado

Photo by Jennifer Odegard

Meet the Quilter

Due to my mother's influence during my childhood near Bemidji, Minnesota, and as part of my 4-H experience, I was a garment sewer from a very early age. Even then I was entering contests—the county fair, the Minnesota State Fair, and the Make It With Wool contest. My mother was a creative sewer and crafter but did not quilt. I didn't start quilting until the 1980s. I took a few classes at the local quilt shop and hand quilted my first few pieces.

After hearing Harriet Hargrave speak at our statewide quilt guild, Colorado Quilting Council, and viewing her trunk show, I was amazed at how she replicated the look of old quilts with a sewing machine. I took her machine quilting class and have never looked back.

For a number of years, I quilted on a regular sewing machine. After retiring from a career as a computer programmer about 12 years ago, I bought a basic Gammill Classic longarm and started a business machine quilting for others. I still quilt on that same machine. Although I enjoy designing, piecing, and machine appliqué, quilting is my favorite part of the process.

I enjoy replicating the look of old quilts using today's techniques—precision cutting, machine piecing, machine appliqué, and machine quilting. I look to old photos for design inspiration, taking my favorite ideas from several quilts. I enjoy the process of drafting a pattern and creating quilting designs. Thanks to inspiration from Karen McTavish, I also like to create traditional-looking wholecloth quilts on my longarm. I tend to quilt very traditionally with feathers and crosshatching. Feathers are my specialty so I challenged myself to create a quilting design for this quilt that contained *no* feathers!

In addition to Harriet Hargrave a number of people have inspired my quilting. Sue Nickels gave me the confidence to do appliqué.

ROSE TRELLIS 62" x 60"

*"Feathers are my specialty so I challenged myself
to create a quilting design with no feathers."*

Trudie Hughes first taught me precision cutting and piecing techniques. Hari Walner and Karen McTavish taught me about machine trapunto.

Quilting has given me so much pleasure that I like to give back by quilting raffle quilts for Colorado Quilting Council and the local Rocky Mountain Quilt Museum. I recently quilted the 30th birthday quilt for the statewide guild.

The most rewarding volunteer project was quilting the top made by students of Platte Canyon High School in Bailey, Colorado, in memory of Emily Keyes. Emily was killed in her school by a gunman who held her, a teacher, and six other students hostage. The quilt top was made as part of the students' healing process and I was honored to quilt it for them. In one border, I quilted the message that Emily texted to her family shortly before she was killed —"I love u guys."

Inspiration and Design

According to historians, the surrender of British General Burgoyne at Saratoga on October 17, 1777, is considered a turning point in the Revolutionary War. The strong diagonal lines formed by the Burgoyne Surrounded blocks reminded me of a trellis. These two things were the inspiration—Burgoyne's surrender created a trellis upon which the United States grew. Since the rose is the national flower, it seemed natural that roses should grow on the trellis.

In keeping with the patriotic nature of the quilt, I selected blue background fabrics. The "red" roses are made from a set of gradated hand-dyed fat quarters. There is even a small amount of white quilting thread.

Nine traditional Burgoyne Surrounded blocks were pieced and the brown inner border was added. Two shades of blue were selected for the background. A brown "wood" fabric was used for the trellis and the narrow inner border.

I created two widths of fabric stems from two different green batiks and cut leaves in three sizes from nine different green batiks. Roses were cut from nine gradated shades of pink/red hand-dyes. Full roses were cut in two sizes as were the rosebuds.

The Burgoyne background was placed on a design wall. As I like symmetry and a well-planned design to work from, the arrangement of stems, roses, and leaves on the background was my first challenge. I had no plan for their placement other than that I wanted the illusion of roses climbing a trellis. I studied photos of a number of rose bushes and rose trellises. My friend Kathy Emmel sent me photos of her gorgeous rose bushes for inspiration.

Starting with about 50 roses and buds, yards of stem, and piles of leaves, I arranged, studied, rearranged, and cut more roses and more piles of leaves. For several days I moved pieces around, got input from my husband (who has a good eye for this!), and cut even more leaves. Finally, I was happy with the arrangement. Leaf colors range from the bluest/darkest in the lower left and get progressively lighter and more yellow as they move up and to the right on the trellis (toward the light source).

The leaves and roses were fused to the background. All edges were stitched down using a machine buttonhole stitch. Stems were "basted" to the background using washable glue and then stitched with a straight stitch close to each edge. Skinny stems were made by couching over eight strands of sewing thread using a zigzag stitch. I used techniques learned from a Sue Nickels' machine appliqué class and from the book *Stitched Raw Edge Appliqué* by Sue and her sister, Pat Holly.

When possible, I like using King Tut™ variegated threads by Superior for buttonhole stitching. The colors change at one inch intervals. The colors endorsed by Sue Nickels are particularly nice as they tend to be shades of a single color. The slight variety in thread color is interesting in the same way as the color variations found in batik and hand-dyed fabrics. An added bonus is that a few thread colors can be used on a large variety of fabrics.

Stitching became my second challenge. Good machine buttonhole stitching involves adjusting the piece in minute increments—sometimes once for every stitch. I feel very comfortable buttonholing an individual block as it is small and easily maneuvered. However, with this project I was manipulating a 50" "block"!

Technique—Quilting the Quilt

As a longarm quilter, the quilting is very important to me and is part of my initial thought process when designing a quilt. I like to leave open areas to showcase quilting.

Designing the Outer Border Quilting Design

For this quilt, I knew I wanted a scalloped outer border that was about 6" wide. As I wanted an even number of scallops on each side, I decided on 10 scallops 5¼" each (fig. 1).

I created a full-size paper pattern of two scallops, leaving about ⅜" to ½" margin to give the design a little breathing room. Starting with a pretty S shape, I played with a design that filled the space nicely and that looked good when placed next to itself (figs. 2–3 on page 62). The quilting design inspiration started with a tiny design on the back of the dollar bill and evolved from there.

For the corners I used a compass to make a nicely rounded smooth corner. Again I started with a full-size pattern of the corner and one swag and modified the quilting design to fill the corners (patterns on page 63).

Marking the Quilt

I darkened the final quilting designs on the paper using a black permanent marker and then used a light box to mark the quilt top. Since the outer border was dark and since the marks needed to stay on the quilt through much handling, I used an iron-off white marking pen. The quilting designs in the blue background were marked using a blue wash-out marker. I took elements of the border quilting design and fit them into the spaces between the appliqué.

Trapunto

To add dimension to the quilt, I used trapunto behind the roses and the quilting motifs in the outer border. The quilt top and a layer of 8-ounce polyester batting were loaded on my longarm machine. I used water-soluble thread to stitch around all of the roses and the quilting motif marked in the outer border, then removed the quilt from the longarm and removed the excess poly batting using sharp scissors and lots of patience.

Quilting

The quilt top, cotton batting, and backing were loaded on the longarm for quilting. I stitched in the ditch around the borders and brown trellis. All roses, stems, and leaves were outlined to make them pop to the foreground. All marked designs in background and outer border were quilted and then loosely echoed. A squiggly woodgrain quilting design was used in the brown trellis and inner border. Veins were quilted in each of the leaves.

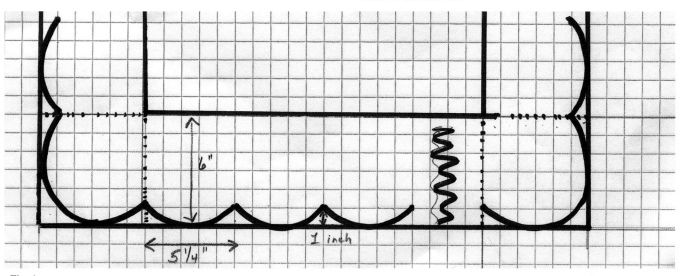

Fig. 1.

Fig. 2.

Fig. 3.

Corner A

Corner B

Finalist
Robin Gausebeck
Rockford, Illinois

Meet the Quilter

It has now been five years since I discovered quilting and when I look back on where I started and how far I've come, I realize what an incredible journey it's been. My first quilt was a simple foundation-pieced quilt that still hangs in my home's entryway, the space for which it was designed. In these five years, I have learned a great many techniques from wonderful teachers, managed to struggle through queen-sized wedding quilts for the two of my children, taught myself hand appliqué, joined a small art quilt group, and become heavily involved in my local guild.

Recently, I have become intrigued with various art media (watercolor pencils, fabric paints, markers, non-toxic dyes) and am looking forward to finding some time to create some of my own fabrics (not that I need any more fabric!). Maybe through the process of making fabric, I will move my quilting in totally unexpected directions. So far, each new quilt that I have designed seemed to be asking me to learn a new technique or skill and I enjoy the challenge of exploring the unknown and learning to trust my instincts.

Mostly, I quilt for myself. I am not overly concerned with whether anyone else likes what I do, as long as I feel that I have succeeded in making art that pleases me. Winning awards always comes as a nice surprise but it doesn't drive my work. However, this is the second quilt of mine that has been named a finalist in this contest and I have to admit, it was *just so cool* to see my quilt hanging in the museum last year.

My husband, Steve, continues to give me great design advice and is a tremendous booster of all my efforts. It really is a privilege to be married to someone who actually looks forward to attending quilt shows with me and who never (or hardly ever) balks at entering a quilt store.

I am lucky to be an early retiree and able to find time to devote to quilting, but there are many other things that interest me as

PUZZLED ABOUT HISTORY 61½" x 74"

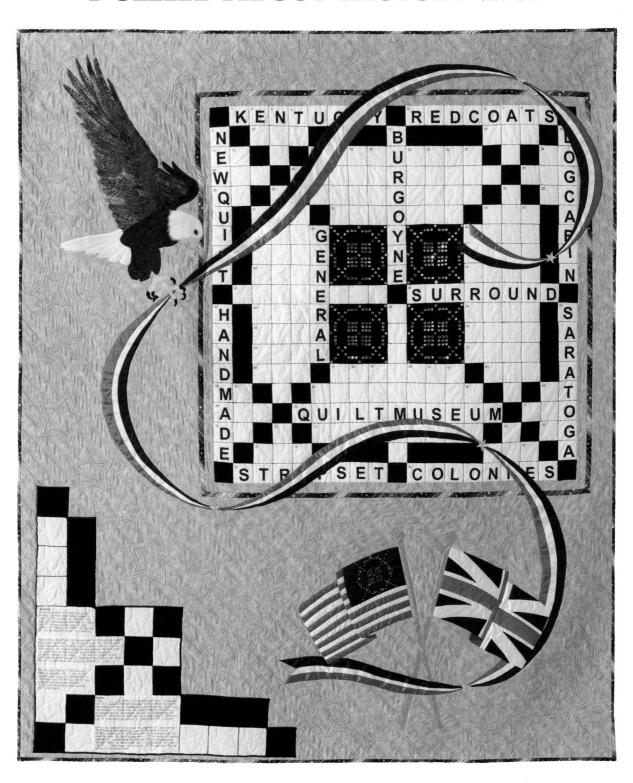

*"The resemblance between the Burgoyne Surrounded block
and a good Sunday crossword was too striking to pass up.
What better way to combine my two passions?"*

well. I sing soprano in my church choir and with the symphony chorale. I love to cook and entertain, am an avid reader, and, of course, I love to solve crossword puzzles. My new super-duper hip joint has enabled me to become active again so I recently took up snowshoeing just in time for the usual winter storms in the upper Midwest.

Design and Inspiration

I am a crossword puzzle addict and have been for many years. The resemblance between the Burgoyne Surrounded block and a good Sunday crossword was too striking to pass up. What better way to combine my two passions?

The selection of a crossword grid as the cornerstone of the quilt, however, presented several challenges. First, where does one find a crossword puzzle that fits the theme? I had to construct one, aiming to use both quilt-related and historical answers and clues. There is computer software that helps in formatting a grid, keeping track of clues, and generally makes the task a little easier. I now have a much greater appreciation for those men and women who are clever enough with words to make sure I have a crossword puzzle to do each morning at the breakfast table.

Choosing to stay with a cohesive theme provided me with the opportunity to learn more about the Battle of Saratoga, in which General John Burgoyne was defeated, or "surrounded," by the American forces led by General Horatio Gates (*not* George Washington, as has sometimes been stated). People who are familiar with the British Union Jack will notice that the flag I used is a slightly different version from the modern one. In 1777, Scotland had not yet been integrated into the United Kingdom; the diagonal red stripes that were added to the flag to mark this unification, therefore, aren't present. As long as I was traveling the historical route, I selected a fabric from Wyndham's Williamsburg line for the back of the quilt.

The last, and perhaps biggest, challenge had to do with construction. I ultimately chose to print the letters on freezer paper-backed fabric with a laser printer, adding a fusible interfacing for more stability. A combination of hand- and machine-appliqué techniques took care of the applied motifs. In making the choice to use some non-traditional fabrics for the flags and banner, I sacrificed ease of construction for visual appeal, a mistake I would like not to make again.

This is not my usual style of quilt. I much prefer abstract, often geometric, quilts that employ vivid colors that I design in a much more intuitive way. I guess I was seduced by the challenge of the crossword puzzle; it must have been a day when the left side of my brain was in control. In the end, the quilt managed to appeal to my head in its cleverness but never quite resonated with me emotionally. The eagle was perhaps the most fun to work on and, in the process, I gained some proficiency in hand appliqué, which will serve me well with future quilts.

Mostly, this was a quilt that was a struggle from start to finish. There was a lot of head-scratching, a lot of "do-overs," and a lot of frustration but, as is usually the case with my quilts, lots of opportunities for learning.

Quilt Design Techniques

The design of a non-traditional quilt is frequently the most difficult aspect of the quilting process. The contemporary quilt may be heavily reliant on irregular, asymmetrical, or non-geometric motifs to create interest and movement. In the traditional quilt, the eye is likely to be attracted to the entire piece and viewed as a pleasing whole; a contemporary or art quilt may depend on the viewer to "create" the impact of the whole by a process where the brain takes disparate parts and brings them together through the power of perception. The desired end result will be a design that has a focal point, movement, and a sense of flow that directs the eye in the way the quiltmaker wishes the quilt to be seen.

There are many excellent sources that explain design principles in easily understood terms. Lyric Kinard's series of essays in *Quilting Arts Magazine* (Issues 25–27) and the books of Katie Pasquini Masopust have been particularly useful for me.

PUZZLED ABOUT HISTORY began with the central concept of the crossword puzzle. Its size (not so small as to be lost and large enough to aid in ease of construction) and the desire for immediate impact dictated its placement in the quilt. To position the grid in the center of the quilt (fig. 1) with a symmetrical field and border attracts the attention of the viewer, but then scatters the eye in a random fashion.

I decided to place the grid in an off-center position because I thought that it would initially catch the viewer off guard. I planned the remaining design elements so that the eye would move from place to place on the quilt in a smooth and unified fashion.

There are many ways to achieve flow and unity of design. Similar shapes or colors strategically located around a quilt lead the eye in a logical pattern. Elements that intersect do much the same thing. In this case, I chose a more obvious method and created a thematically unifying element—the red, white, and blue banner, which both literally and figuratively connects the quilt's disparate motifs (fig. 2).

Not only does the choice of colors reflect a patriotic play on the presumed inspiration for the Burgoyne Surrounded block, but it serves as a unifying element by physically connecting the eagle, which holds the banner in its talons, to the Revolutionary War era flags of the American and British forces. At the same time, the use of the small gold stars at the points where the banner "folds" echoes the star motifs, which have been quilted into the background and repeat the gold color of the flagpoles.

When I begin to design a new quilt, whether it is representational, thematic, or abstract in feel, there are several questions I almost always ask myself:
• What idea am I trying to convey to the viewer of this quilt?
• What are the most important elements that will facilitate this idea? The selection of colors, repetition of design elements, and the flow of shapes, values, or hues are all points to consider.
• How can I arrange these elements to create a pleasing whole that grabs and holds the viewer's interest?

When I am in left-brain mode, these are some of my design considerations. When I'm in right-brain mode, I just throw some fabrics up on my design wall and see what works and what doesn't. Both methods work for me and help to create quilts that, I hope, please my most demanding critic—me.

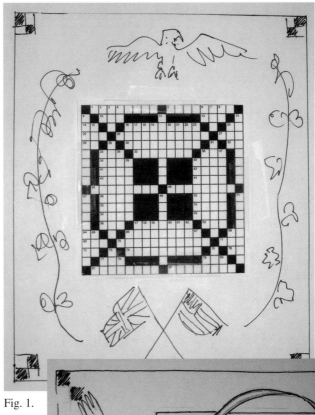

Fig. 1.

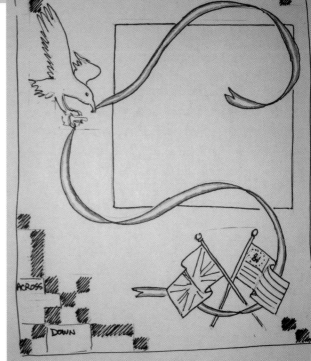

Fig. 2.

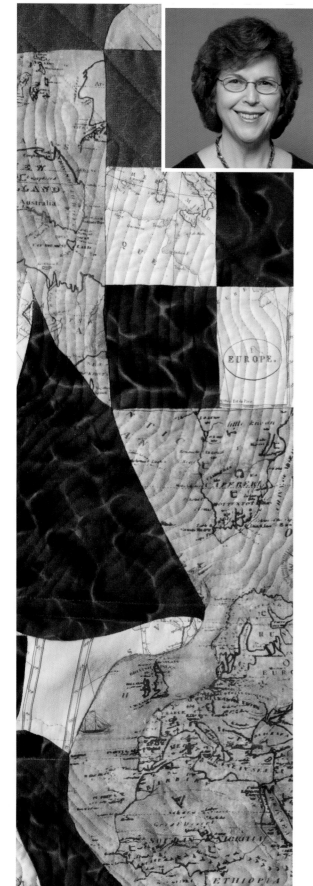

Photo by John K. Hobbs

Finalist

Patricia Hobbs

Macomb, Illinois

Meet the Quilter

My great-grandmother was a seamstress for a Swiss tailor. My grandmother and her two daughters quilted. As a child, I had the neighborhood girls hand-dying fabrics using watercolors and trading fabrics. At age eight, I knew about fabric remnants. My mother worked for a large department store, and I made quick friends with the ladies in the drapery department. It was a place lush with boxes of scraps.

The city library had wonderful books about quilts. The TV aired shows about homemaking skills. I entertained myself with sewing. My first quilt (unfinished to date) was an English paper-pieced Grandmother's Flower Garden pattern that I had found in one book.

Eventually, I found the visual arts and became an art teacher. While I still do watercolors and show those regularly, I am enjoying all of the innovative fiber art possibilities. I joke about being Grandma Moses in reverse. She began needling her images and later turned to oil painting because it was quicker. I began with painting and turned to fiber art after I retired. Many of my watercolors would make colorful quilt designs, although I don't like doing anything twice. It doesn't take much to inspire me, but I have found ideas when I am traveling, reading, gardening, etc. I try to keep my eyes wide open, and I enjoy exploring new techniques and ideas.

Even when I worked more than full-time as a teacher, I saved midnight to one o'clock for creating—never working after two o'clock as things go weird after that hour.

I enjoy making crazy quilts because there are no rules. Rusting, dyeing, dispersing dye, and painting are some of the methods of manipulating fabric that I enjoy. Line drawings on used tea bags that may be attached to fabric with acrylic mat medium and other paper ephemeral pieces have found their way onto my quilts. Beads and other small objects are sewn on, too. I have been

GENTLEMAN JOHNNY 52½" x 55"

*"I taught calligraphy for 34 years. It is more difficult
to do on cloth with a plain marking pen."*

making a series of smaller quilts to try out my ideas. Many of my quilts are about my family members and genealogy. I enjoy using old photographic images on quilts.

Inspiration and Design

I always take time to visit The National Quilt Museum when I am in Paducah. The last time I was walking through the vestibule, the red color on a brochure caught my eye. As I was looking at it, one of the staff members asked if I was planning to try the New Quilts from an Old Favorite challenge. Halfway laughing, I answered, "Oh, sure."

The Burgoyne Surrounded block was new to me. The computer was a quick and easy way to find out about the block and its origin. Each tidbit of information led me down the path towards a finished quilt.

The first step was to place twenty of the blocks together on a sheet of paper to see what an original quilt would have looked like. It represented a great deal of piecing for anyone, and it resembled a coverlet pattern. I then distorted one block on the computer in every way I

could think of including a bull's-eye or target, but the phrase "the pattern should be recognizable" brought me back to one design.

Most of the fabrics used in this quilt were fresh from Hancocks of Paducah. I have often said that I used whatever was on top of the pile, but this was just another logical choice and a push to keep me going. If I'd had to search out these specific fabrics I might have lost momentum.

Because I had distorted the block, a paper pattern was necessary to keep it all accurate. I decided to keep the distortion going to the very edges, which made the binding a bit of a challenge (fig. 1). Since the General's story was so interesting, I felt it must be included on the borders. I probably won't do any more with this particular block, but it might be fun to try this method with other quilt blocks and even piece several together into a larger quilt.

Technique Essay

In the whole process of quiltmaking, designing the piece is the most enjoyable for me. Of course, hunting

Fig. 1.

a fabric with beautiful colors or patterns is high up on the list. Quilting a piece has been a slow learning curve for me. Buying a top-of-the-line home sewing machine has improved the quality of my stitching along with practice, practice, practice.

I taught calligraphy for 34 years. It is more difficult to do on cloth with a plain marking pen—no chisel edge pen nib (fig. 2). I believe that every process learned could be applied to or used in quilting.

I used the Adobe® Photoshop® Elements Essentials program to manipulate the scanned image of the original block. One copy was printed on an 8½" x 11" sheet of paper on which notes were made and measurements were figured (fig. 3).

My printer will take 10" wide paper, so with the design on the computer screen and using the ruler grids, one small section at a time could be cropped out and printed. Each piece was one twenty-fifth of the whole design. The pieces were numbered as they were printed and then taped together. Lines that were fuzzy from enlarging were traced with a black marker (fig. 4).

The pattern could then be cut apart piece by piece and traced onto fabric. I made notes on each piece as to its position and color.

Pieces were either set in by machine or by hand.

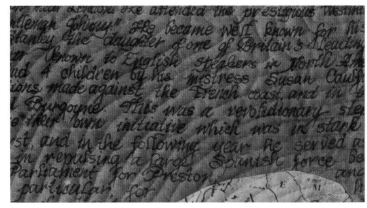

Fig. 2.

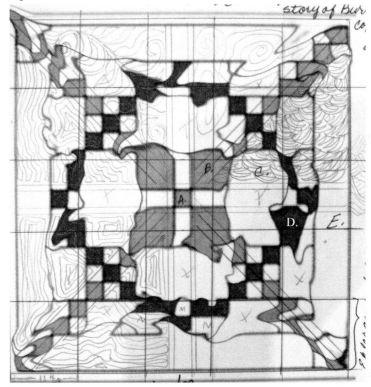

Fig. 3.

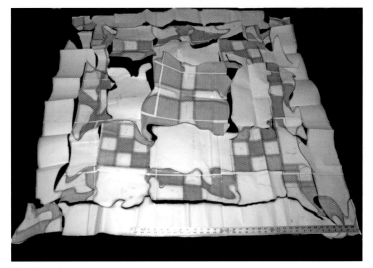

Fig. 4.

Finalist
Barbara Holtzman
Holyoke, Colorado

Meet the Quilter

While I have been sewing all of my life, quilting is relatively new to me. Coming from a family of all girls, we learned early about sewing—from Mom, from 4-H, from home ec classes. All my sisters and I enjoy having some kind of creative outlet, whether it's crocheting, scrapbooking, or cross-stitching. I've done most of those, but when I got the quilting bug, everything else was left by the wayside. I still have plans to complete my kids' scrapbooks, but they may be having kids of their own before I'm done!

Quilting fulfills a creative outlet for me in a medium I'm comfortable with. I can be creative with the fabric and technique and choose a traditional pattern or create my own design. I find I can be precise or loose, traditional or creative.

It's interesting how our individual backgrounds shape our style. I have friends whose quilts really reflect the types of people they are with the color palettes and styles of quilt they choose to do. I never used to think I had my own style. With every quilt I try a new technique or challenge myself in some way. I think if I try all the techniques, eventually one will resonate with me and I'll have a direction I want to explore more in depth. Until that time, I'm having fun finding my own style.

I can tell just by my fabric choices that I really do have somewhat of a style of my own, or at least one that seems to be developing. As I look back on quilts I've made I see colors and shapes that I have repeated. When I have two choices of the same color, I tend to lean towards the truer, clearer color. Looking at designs, I seem to pick clean, simple lines and bold shapes. I think it has something to do with growing up in the 70s and the pop culture that was around me. I remember all the graffiti and bold colors. Whatever the reason, "I yam what I yam," as Popeye would say!

The quilting world has so many things going on right now. It's always fun to get on the Internet and see what other quilters

WILDFLOWERS 57½" x 57½"

"I seem to pick clean, simple lines and bold shapes. I think it has to do with growing up in the 70s and the pop culture that was around me."

are doing. That, too, shapes how I look at quilting. I enjoy trying new techniques. I'd like to try an art quilt sometime. I think I'm secretly a quilt artist-wanna-be!

Inspiration and Design

Every quilter enjoys that feeling of accomplishment when fabric choice, design creativity, quilting, and effort all come together in their own special quilt. I find myself constantly trying to do what this book is all about—taking a traditional pattern and trying to reinvent it creatively. Instead of starting with a technique, I decide on the quilt I want to do and then research the best technique to get the look I want. I love the challenge that this contest creates for me.

The Burgoyne block is a fairly straightforward block—all squares and rectangles. When I first looked at this design I thought I would "pull it" in each direction and get the same block but distorted. I worked and worked with it and couldn't get anything that clicked for me until I decided that I could turn it into a flower. Suddenly it all seemed to come together and make sense. I like the order of multiples so it was a natural choice to reproduce the flower block four times.

I tried to use colors from the opposite ends of the spectrum. I knew green would be the background color—these are flowers in a field after all—so I chose reds, oranges, yellows, and pinks. I found a terrific grassy green in my stash and pulled all the other colors I thought would brighten the green. Some I had in my stash and others, of course, I had to go shopping for! Even then some had to be pulled out. I think everyone has the ability to choose what's right for them. I tried to listen to my own inner feelings and choose what felt right for this quilt.

Techniques

For this quilt I used a freezer-paper sewing technique I really enjoyed. The pattern is drawn out full-scale and cut apart for the templates, which are ironed onto the back of the selected fabrics. Seam allowances on pieces that overlap others are brushed with starch and pressed under with a hot dry iron. Pieces are then overlapped and stitched together with a very small zigzag stitch.

To make the flower block, enlarge the pattern 200% (page 75). Trace the pattern on the dull side of freezer paper. Transfer all markings. Carefully cut out each pattern piece and iron onto the back side of the selected fabrics.

With a small brush, wet the curved outside edges of pieces 1, 3, 5, and 7 with starch. Press the curved edges under using a hot, dry iron (fig. 1).

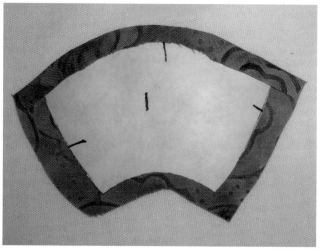

Fig. 1.

Using a light box, line up pieces 1 and 2. Use a pin or a piece of tape to temporarily hold the pieces together. Join with a very small zigzag stitch (fig. 2).

Fig. 2.

Repeat for the other three petals. Starch, turn under, and press the sides of each petal (fig. 3).

Fig. 3.

Starch and press the middle circle. Lay out all the pieces as shown (fig. 4).

Fig. 4.

Again using the light box, line up each piece with a corner and sew a petal and corner together. Join the remaining sections together. Finally, sew on the middle of the flower (fig. 5).

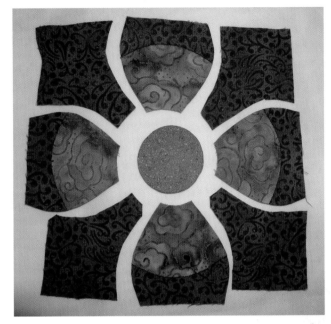

Fig. 5.

Tip: I made my own light box. Cut a hole in the lower side of a cardboard box that you can slide a small lamp into. Place a piece of glass on the top and you're set! I like to use the compact fluorescent bulbs; they don't get hot like a regular bulb.

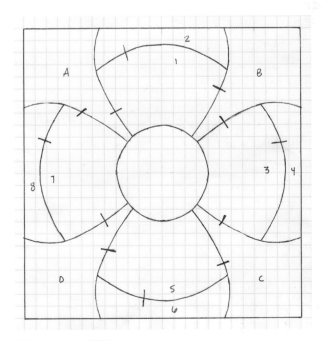

Enlarge pattern 200%

Finalist

Chris Lynn Kirsch
Watertown, Wisconsin

& Sharon Rotz
Mosinee, Wisconsin

The Collabration

Chris: This is our third collaborative quilt to be accepted as a finalist in the NQOF contest. We share equally in the designing, construction, and quilting and find great joy in working together and inspiring one another.

Sharon: We all strive to live in harmony and balance. We find harmony in the bold lines of tall, straight trunks of trees growing in a row, balanced by the small curving shapes of fluttering leaves. We find harmony in a round blazing Aztec sun balanced by glowing beams radiating from its center. When I met Chris, I found a quilter who balances me. When one of us hits that point of frustration and non-inspiration, the other rises to the occasion and completes the idea.

Meet Sharon

Sewing was a part of my life from the time I was ten years old and I joined a local 4-H club. My first sewing experience was on the treadle machine of my sewing leader. Coordinating the motions of both my hands and my feet was quite a challenge (perhaps not unlike the coordination of hand and foot speed I use in my free-motion quilting today). Because of my love for fabric and sewing, I pursued a degree in home economics education.

Raising a young family, I used my sewing skills in a home-based business creating and altering clothing and home decor. The mother of my daughter's friend introduced me to quilting, and my sewing machine hasn't been idle since. I remember the cardboard template I used to cut squares for my first quilt. Now with my collection of rotary cutters, rulers, and mats, I certainly accomplish more in a fraction of the time.

Soon I was enjoying teaching and sharing my love of quilting with others. It was on a quilting retreat that I met Chris. We formed an instant connection and went home inspired to make our first quilt together. This would be more easily accomplished

GOYNE ROUND IN CIRCLES 58" x 58"

"We share equally in the design, construction, and quilting and find great joy in working together and inspiring one another."

if we lived closer together, but we happen to live half a state apart. Undeterred, we have managed to make several quilts together despite the distance and our busy teaching schedules. I feel blessed to have such a quilting friend.

Today my quilting teeters on the fence, half falling in the category of traditional and half falling into art quilts. I love making creative projects, exploring new ideas, and playing with color and fabric choices. After creative time, I find the need to fall back into the structure and timeless appeal of a more traditional quilt. I continue to share my quilts and quilting experience with others through teaching, designing patterns, and writing quilting books.

Even though my first sewing machine is worn and gone, as are several others, my passion for making quilts still abounds and someday they will be taking my scissors away as I cut up the bed sheets at the nursing home.

Meet Chris

My sewing addiction also began as a child. My mother taught me to sew when I was seven and home economics (at least the sewing part) was my favorite subject throughout school. I changed direction in college and became a dental hygienist. Although I enjoyed my career, it didn't feed my need to create. In 1987 my sister-in-law talked me into taking a quilting class and that's when I found my niche. I began as a very traditional quilter and this has evolved into a passion for contemporary and art quilts. I love it all!

I've retired from dentistry and am blessed with the opportunity to quilt full time. I teach at two local technical colleges, for quilt shows and guilds throughout the country, and lead quilting cruises in the US and Europe. My classes range from very traditional (hand quilting) to encouraging students to find the artist within. I've also written two books. I'm so grateful to the Lord for giving me the abilities and opportunities to do what I love; my faith has become a very great inspiration in my quilting.

Meeting Sharon was a huge boost to my creativity. Even though we are separated by distance, we are connected by our quilting passion, joy-filled friendship,

Fig. 1.

and mutual faith. I feel I truly grow when collaborating with Sharon because she is incredibly talented and this pushes me to do my very best. It is amazing to create together what neither of us could do individually. It is also helpful to be able to send a current quilt to her when none of my ideas are working.

Sharon and I share much more than a love for quilting. We both have very supportive husbands, two married children, and beautiful grandchildren. We both live in log homes in the woods of Wisconsin and share a wacky sense of humor. We've been known to polka together at quilting events. We are so very blessed. Life is to be enjoyed!

Inspiration and Design
Chris

I was the one to begin the quilt this time. My first thought was to play with the fabric placement in the traditional Burgoyne Surrounded block so that new patterns would emerge. Soon I realized how many small squares and rectangles needed to be pieced. Even though I enjoy piecing, it "seamed" a bit overwhelming.

I began to think that turning the different sized squares into various sizes of fused circles would be a lot more fun. By using Caryl Bryer Fallert's Gradations fabric, I could get all the different values of colors from one piece of yardage (which now looks like Swiss cheese).

Finding a background was a bit of a challenge. After much trial and error, a hand-dyed piece I had splurged on in Paducah last spring caught my eye and it was just right. I fused the circles, layered the sandwich, and did some minor quilting, deciding I would add quilt-as-you-go borders later. "Later" never happened as I went through a mind melt and couldn't decide what to do next. At this point I called Sharon and yelled, "HELP!"

Inspiration and Design
Sharon

When I saw the colorful center Chris had made, I knew what I would like to try for a border. Building on her idea of changing the square shapes of the traditional block into circles, I saw the opportunity to balance these colorful circles with a border of straight lines radiating out from the center.

Fig. 2.

I love the look of scrap quilts but in this case, I felt that numerous fabrics would compete with rather than complement the center. Various commercially printed monotone fabrics seemed to provide the best balance. As often happens, I was moving a pile of unrelated fabrics when one caught my eye and suddenly I was pulling out every yellow and blue that I had in my stash. My heart was singing as I knew these would be the colors for the border.

Again building off the idea of harmony and balance, the quilting designs started to take shape in my mind. To balance the contemporary look of the quilt, I tried a slightly updated version of a traditional fleur-de-lis design in the shape of a cross in the imagined sashing. As I was searching for design possibilities, I came across a trapunto design by Helen Squire in the Fall 2005 issue of *American Quilter*. I used this as the initial inspiration, then played with and reshaped it to suit my thoughts for our quilt.

Techniques

Border—Sharon

I laid out full-size paper patterns for each of the four borders. On these preliminary paper patterns, I played with the border width, size, and shape. Rays with varying widths of approximately 1"–2" seemed pleasing. Varying the lengths of each inner ray was more eye-catching than a smooth inner border. Curving the outer edge of the border unit added interest and harmony with the circles. Continuing the rays around the corners proved to be better than mitering, which led to choppy angles.

When I was happy with the border design, I traced each of the four borders onto freezer paper. I numbered each ray and each section of each ray. Each of the rays was then cut apart and laid in position on the quilt. I gathered my numerous yellows and oranges for the inner rays. Dark blues were chosen for the outer rays to accentuate the center of the quilt and frame the lively inner border. By keeping the colors closely related and the patterns monotone or subtle, the borders would have a scrappy yet unified look, complementing the hand-dyed fabric used in the center.

After cutting, the freezer-paper templates were pressed to the wrong side of the fabrics and cut with ¼" seam

Fig. 3.

allowance. The differing fabric patterns and colors were dispersed around the borders (figs. 1–2, pages 78–79). By laying each ray section back in place after attaching the fabric, I checked the color and fabric distribution. Then each blue outer ray was matched and stitched to its yellow or orange inner ray. The rays were stitched together in sections, and the sections into the four borders. They were added in the same manner that you would add mitered borders to your quilt (fig. 3, page 80).

Circles—Chris

In order to cut gradations of circles, I fused Wonder Under® paper-backed fusible web to the wrong side of the entire piece of rainbow fabric and used the Olfa® Rotary Circle Cutter to cut circles of various sizes.

One of the wonderful things about challenges is trying new things and learning what works, what doesn't, and how you'd do it better next time. Please learn along with us. The fused circles in the center of the quilt were cut from a commercially printed fabric, while the circles in the border came from hand-dyed fabric. The hand-dyed fabric has a tighter weave with a higher thread count. All the circles looked great at first, but as the quilting and finishing was being done, the inner circles began to "fuzz" around the edges (fig. 4). But since the quilt was so exciting as a whole, we chose to embrace it all as is. But next time….

For the circle placement, I folded the square of background fabric in half horizontally, vertically, and on both diagonals, and pressed creases in. After opening the fabric flat I marked all the lines with a sliver of soap, my favorite marker—it shows up on all but the lightest fabrics and always comes out. I laid out the circles for the first block in the upper left square, working until the block looked even and balanced. Now I knew where the additional horizontal, vertical, and diagonal lines needed to be for the subsequent circles to fit. I drew lines across the rest of the background and laid out the remaining blocks. After every circle was laid out correctly, I carefully pressed everything in place.

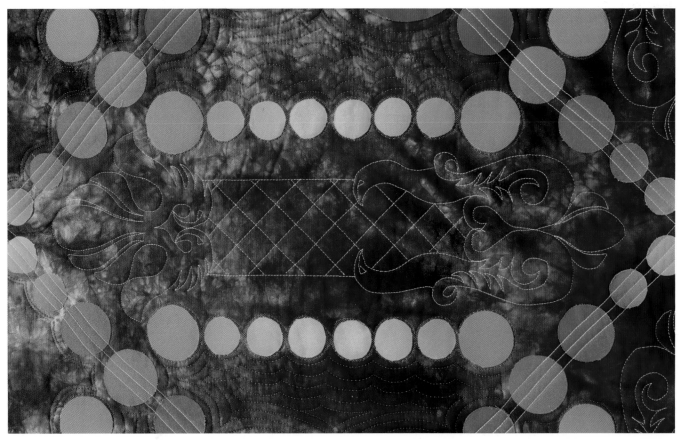

Fig. 4.

Finalist
Ann L. Petersen
Aurora, Colorado

Meet the Quilter

When I was a child, my mother sewed many of my dresses and I remember sitting on the floor by the sewing machine and playing with the scraps. I sewed an organdy skirt for my Barbie® doll by hand-gathering it to a scrap of elastic. You can imagine what it looked like! Not the lovely, elegant skirt I had envisioned, but I kept it for years and in an odd way it was always an inspiration to learn the techniques that make finished items look nice.

When I was in junior high school, my maternal grandmother, Bertha Miller, would have me come to stay on the ranch for one week in late summer and we would sew my new school wardrobe. The shopping trip to buy fabric before we started was always a highlight of the summer. Grandma was a very good seamstress and I learned a lot from both her and my mom. My mother never has quilted and Grandma never quilted when I knew her. I have a quilt she made for Mom and Dad as a wedding present, an appliqué quilt that was quilted by her church group, but that was one of the last quilts she ever worked on.

My father's mother loved patchwork and always had several quilts in process right up to her death in the early 1970s. Both grandmothers taught me to love and appreciate the craft and art of needlework of all types and I believe they would be proud of their contributions to my accomplishments today. I work as a quilt designer, both of my own quilts and for a local quilt shop, Great American Quilt Factory. I sew all day on quilts for the business and go home in the evening eager to work on my own designs.

Inspiration and Design

Three years ago one of my neighbors up the street put a hanging flower basket out on their front porch, which contained only some pinky-orange petunias and some deep blue-violet lobelia. I found the color combination to be stunning and decided immediately to make a quilt using those colors. By the time I took my camera up the street to capture the colors, the flowers

SARATOGA CAMPFIRES 66" x 66"

*"Both my grandmothers taught me to love and appreciate the craft
and art of needlework of all types and I believe they would be proud
of their contributions to my accomplishments today."*

had faded and other flowers had bloomed; but that first image stuck in my mind.

About that time I took a Log Cabin class from Flavin Glover at Quilt Colorado. I used fabrics of those blue-violets and orange-pinks. The quilt never got further along than five or so 5" blocks, but throughout this past year I played with the idea of using them in a Burgoyne Surrounded quilt. The design and construction evolved in a completely different direction, but the colors remained as the only element from the original design.

From the first time I knew that this year's block was to be Burgoyne Surrounded, I felt that I might skip making an entry for this year's contest. Timing was bad, due to many other obligations I had taken on, and the block seemed boring with lots of empty space. In the end, it was the empty space that became the emphasis of the design.

In mid-September, with my obligations complete, I was about to undergo some surgery. I decided to sit down one evening with graph paper and a picture of the Burgoyne Surrounded block to see if I could design something I could get a good start on before my surgery date. After several false tries, I decided to make just one Burgoyne Surrounded block, but increase the size by 400% and add piecing to the large background spaces.

Curves appealed to me because the block was very static and all straight lines. The curved spikes were easy to design and gave the quilt a more dynamic quality. The next day, I pulled my old selection of fabrics and arranged them light to dark in each colorway.

I decided to make the elements of the original block very subtle by using a monochromatic color scheme with only the dark and light blue-violets with a counterpoint of the more colorful pink spikes. I graded the values from lightest fabrics in the center to darkest along the border. This technique always adds a special luminosity to a design and is one of my favorite things to do.

As I worked on the quilt, I found myself going repeatedly to my fabric stash and pulling more fabric in each color range to give the quilt more depth and variety. I am a firm believer that the more fabrics in a quilt, the better the finished quilt will be. The two colors range in value from light to dark with many, many fabrics of approximately the same value.

I started cutting squares from the blues and was piecing by noon. I was able to piece most of the top in the week before surgery. All of the curved blocks were paper pieced. Instead of printing out a sheet of paper for each pieced block segment, I just traced one of each different pattern onto freezer paper and used them over and over—an ecologically friendly method, and you don't have to tear off all the little bits of paper at the end. You simply press a section of the freezer paper to the fabric, fold back along the sewing line, and sew next to the fold instead of through the paper.

I was tired the week after being released from the hospital but found I could sew in shorter segments of time and then rest. It was two weeks before I was allowed to drive and return to work, so the quilt gave me a good way to work on my returning stamina.

After the borders were added, the quilt still needed an additional element to look complete so I decided to add some appliqué. As I had worked on the piecing, the pink spikes began to look like campfires glowing in the blue-violet night. One day when I was too tired to sew, I Googled Burgoyne-Campfires, thinking about what I would name the quilt. I came across several mentions of General Burgoyne leaving his campfires burning the night before the Battle of Saratoga so that he could remove his troops from a suspected attack by the Americans.

The history also mentioned that the forests of upstate New York were so thick that Burgoyne had real difficulties moving his troops, which helped contribute to his defeat. Thinking of the thick forests, I decided to add a branch of appliquéd leaves across the top of the quilt and another partial branch to the right side. This also gave me my clue as to how to quilt the piece.

The appliqué leaf pattern was taken from a leaf on a bush in my front yard. I traced around the leaf several dozen times directly onto the paper side of my fusible web, then cut out the centers of each tracing, leaving about ⅜" of fusible around the edge of each to maintain softness in the finished product. The resulting fusible web, which looks a lot like Swiss cheese, is then ironed onto the wrong side of the leaf fabric. The leaves are cut on the drawn line and fused in place. I used three different fabrics for the leaves (figs. 1–3).

The stem piece was cut from a ⅞" bias strip of fabric, pressed in half lengthwise, then sewn along the raw edges with a very narrow seam allowance (less than ¼") (fig. 4). The folded edge was then pressed over the seam and appliquéd by hand along the final long edge.

To quilt the borders, I drew more of the stem and leaf design around all four sides and quilted it with a variegated thread in a lighter blue color. To quilt the lighter blue squares that make up the Burgoyne Surrounded block, I made a reduced copy of my leaf to fit the diagonal of each smaller square making up the light blue block. The rest of the quilt was quilted with free-motion leaves of various kinds in several different shades of blue thread.

When the quilt was done I realized that everything I used (fabrics, batting, cording, thread, paper, fusible web) came from my stash. I only purchased one spool of thread when I ran out of the color I was using in the bobbin. I even found a lovely piece of backing in my stash that had been purchased for another quilt. It was the same as one of the fabrics I had used in the border and the body of the quilt. I didn't start out to make a quilt entirely from my stash, but since I was confined at home, it was wonderful to be able to draw on my very nice collection of quilting fabrics and supplies.

Fig. 1.

Fig. 3.

Fig. 2.

Fig. 4.

Photo by Colleen Kemp

Finalist
Cathy Pilcher Sperry
West Chester, Ohio

Meet the Quilter

I won the parent jackpot! My parents believed in me and nurtured me to believe in myself. They encouraged not only faith, education, good health, and time and money management, but also creativity. They taught me to not be confined by what I thought were my limitations, but to go after my dreams in spite of them. Mom taught me to sew quite young and we made all our clothes. Dad has always been our greatest fan and cheerleader. My brothers humored us as we pursued our passion.

I have been quilting for over 20 years. It seemed to be a natural progression from 4-H and competitive clothing construction in high school, to a home economics education degree from Oregon State University, to teaching high school, to becoming a stay-at-home mom. Now that our children are grown, I find myself with more creative thoughts and ideas than I will ever have time to complete.

I do try to get as much studio time as I can into my week, but the majority of my attention is now directed towards the business that my husband, Dave, and I own and operate in Cincinnati (www. speedprocinci.com). Speedpro Imaging is a large format premium digital printing and design business. It has been fun and gratifying to see Dave's consumer packaging/food industry background and my teaching, design, and quilting skills come to life in a new arena.

The most important part of quilting to me, in addition to my family, is meeting the other exceptional people who have crossed my path. Dave and I were in the corporate world for nearly 30 years, which took us around the country. In most instances it was quilting that opened doors to new friendships, experiences, and opportunities for me. I have had the privilege of being a featured quilter, presenting quilting programs to community groups and organizations, as well as teaching my passion for quilting to others in different regions of the United States.

Due to time constraints, I find myself working on a much smaller scale, putting more techniques into fewer pieces. We have down-sized our home and likewise, I have down-sized my studio. I use

THE HAPPINESS IN MY HANDS 69½" x 58"

"I like to take triangular shapes and add further interest by dividing them into three parts, using light, medium, and dark values of the same color."

what I have and only shop when absolutely necessary. This has been a cleansing as well as a freeing experience and it forces me to be more creative with what I have to work with. I am very thankful for this journey and have learned that I really need very little.

Inspiration and Design

I am most inspired by God's beautiful creations and the words and people he puts in my daily walk. Such was the day in early spring that I found myself jotting down thoughts on a Sunday morning. I was recovering from an arm injury that had left me unable to do anything with my hands. The words that morning spoke about the importance of our hands; how they heal, hold, comfort, nurture, and create. They bring happiness to others. This was my inspiration for the first piece to be made following five months of therapy and it played a major part in the healing of my arms.

Inspiration leads me to designing and I begin to think about some of the essentials of composition. I don't always center my design. Curves, particularly S-curves, are appealing to the eye. They help move the eye across the surface of the design and give the feeling of movement. Triangular shapes are pleasing and interesting compositionally and are a nice contrast to the curves. I like to take those triangular shapes and add further interest by dividing them into three parts, using light, medium, and dark values of the same color. I did this with the Flying Geese, in addition to varying their sizes.

I pay attention to the foreground and background to give the illusion of layers and to draw the viewer in for a closer look. Make that close inspection worth the effort by offering details such as bobbin work, sequins and beads, piping, and precision piecing. The details can make an ordinary quilt sing!

I used trapunto for the first time on THE HAPPINESS IN MY HANDS. Large open areas were planned in the master design for this technique, which plays off the dimensional, pieced sections. I added bobbin work with Razzle Dazzle™ thread around the center motif for more definition on that portion of trapunto. One less layer of polyester batt was used as I worked from the center out to make the center of the Burgoyne Surrounded block more pronounced. The

center has four layers (fig. 1); the first feather wreath has three layers; the corded circle has four layers again, and the outermost feather wreath has two layers.

Fig. 1.

Technique

When I begin designing a new quilt I have a list of techniques and design elements in mind. I also think about the colors I want to use and have some of the fabrics pulled for inspiration. I begin with basic shapes and then go back and divide and subdivide so I have areas to create dimension using value.

In THE HAPPINESS IN MY HANDS I started with the Burgoyne Surrounded block. I wanted a feeling of elevation, so I divided each square and rectangle of the basic design into eight parts. This gave me the areas to use light, medium, and dark batiks to create the illusion of elevation. I planned ahead to use batiks because of their unique properties—the accuracy with which I am able to piece tiny pieces and the ability to get a small block with many seams to lie flat. The variation in shades and value throughout a single piece of batik can create sparkle from block to block.

I placed the Burgoyne Surrounded block on 60" x 60" white design paper and worked out from the off-centered setting, keeping my list of design elements in mind. I left large open areas for trapunto, quilting, and embellishment. Having a master design is an invaluable tool during construction. I often go back to measure positions and locations to get components placed correctly.

The wave design that curves around the center block was machine appliquéd with batiks. Using my master, I traced the design onto the backing paper of fusible web.

It was trimmed to within ⅛" of the cutting line. This keeps the area soft because only ⅛" of fusible adhesive remains around the edge of the appliquéd design. The prepared wave was fused to the background fabric and then stitched with a machine buttonhole stitch using a variegated trilobal polyester thread (fig. 2).

The Flying Geese design is freeform and each section was a little different, necessitating its own set of templates. I traced them onto Strathmore® Paper Palette from the master design. Each one was labeled with the section number, value positions, and grain lines (fig. 3). They were then cut apart and fused to the RIGHT side of each fabric, leaving enough space between pieces to be trimmed with a ¼" seam allowance (fig. 4). A little more allowance was added to the outside edges of the background pieces for hand piecing.

The paper was left on throughout the piecing process and was used as a guide to match up all the points. It makes for very accurate piecing on Y-seams and odd shaped pieces. As each Flying Geese block was completed, it was pressed, trimmed, and labeled with its number position in the design. When the blocks were sewn into one long curved section, I stitched from the point side of each one so I had better control over the points. The Flying Geese strip was hand pieced into the design, working from the center out, again for control of the 56 points (fig. 5).

I photograph my quilt top and print out 8" x10" copies to practice drawing quilting and trapunto designs. Then I put tracing paper over my master and draw them out full size. The trapunto designs are transferred to the quilt top. All other quilting was done free motion, using the drawing as a guide.

Before I begin to quilt, I always make samples with the EXACT materials I plan to use. I label all the information—threads, machine settings, needles, feet, and so on—on the actual samples for future reference. In addition to this, I keep a notebook at my machine when I am working so that I can record thoughts, materials, and technique notes for each project. I can refer back to this on future projects and it gives me a starting point, rather than having to go back to the beginning each time. These work methods are huge time savers.

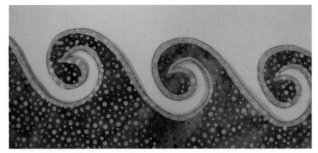
Fig. 2.

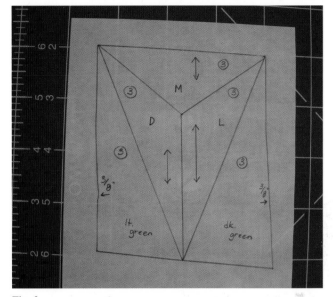
Fig. 3.

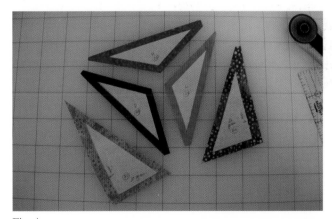
Fig. 4.

Fig. 5.

BURGOYNE SURROUNDED: New Quilts from an Old Favorite

Finalist
Mary Sue Suit
Sidney, Nebraska
& Judy Woodworth
Gering, Nebraska

Meet the Quilters
Mary Sue Introduces the Quilters

BRILLIANT BLIZZARD represents the combined effort of two friends. Judy executed the wonderful quilting around the design I created and sewed. Both of us squeeze the maximum amount of quilting time into busy lives that also include husbands, grown children, grandchildren, and pets. I have been quilting for more years than I am willing to admit to, but was lucky enough to meet Judy about eleven years ago.

Judy was just beginning her quilting journey when she purchased a longarm machine with the confidence that a custom quilting service could be her new job. It did not take long for her and others to realize that she had indeed found her calling. A wonderful designer in her own right, she is a powerhouse of energy and talent, which she enjoys sharing. Judy has a busy schedule quilting for clients but manages to allow me to work in partnership with her for a quilt or two a year. She has recently begun teaching at national events, sharing her abilities and designs.

Finding inspiration in life itself, she is often seen with her camera snapping pictures for future reference. Somehow she finds time to create show quilts of her own as well as working with a partner who is always pushing the deadline.

My fascination with geometric quilts began when it was more popular for girls to be burning their bras than doing any kind of sewing. The quilting won out when I just started putting fabric together. What more did you need but a sewing machine, fabric, and a basement? An essentially self-taught quiltmaker, I have devised my own piecing techniques for working with the family of angles that includes the 45-degree kaleidoscope triangle. Since I consider "template" a four letter word, I have perfected quick and strip-piecing techniques for most of my piecing, some of which have been shared in technique-oriented books.

Fabric and a geometric shape usually spark my creative engine. Letting the fabric speak first, I cut pieces and put them up on the

Brilliant Blizzard 68½" x 68½"

*"One of Diana's beautiful snowflakes floated to the quilt top, turning
the colors into the northern lights and thus the blizzard began."*

design wall. Starting the design in the middle of the quilt, I let it grow as it will. I never know when it starts where or how it will end. It works for me but it takes a partner with the patience of Job to deal with my "design process."

Design and Inspiration
Mary Sue

One sure fact about my life and quilting is that no matter what the plan, one thing always leads to another. The creation of BRILLIANT BLIZZARD was no exception. Life led me to quilting, quilting led me to Judy, and Judy led me to entering quilt contests. For several years we have thought about entering the New Quilts from an Old Favorite contest, but could not fit the project into our schedules. When I realized in early October that Burgoyne Surrounded was the block, I immediately knew the format I wanted to follow.

I knew from experience that one large starburst superimposed on four Burgoyne Surrounded blocks would work and should be no problem. Piecing the star went fairly smoothly, but working with solid fabrics for the first time in many years proved to be a relearning experience. (I have a partner to this star waiting for an ugly block contest.)

I told Judy piecing the Burgoyne block would be easy, but sewing the little squares turned into the biggest challenge of the piecing process. I have since instructed Judy to drop what she is doing, drive to where I am, and hit me with a baseball bat the next time I tell her something "will be easy."

The solid squares were arranged to flow around the starburst following the colors within the star. It was not until the quilt top was in one piece that I stepped away from the design wall and said, "Wow! It does look good." The bold graphic design sprang off the wall and brought a smile to my face. It is so nice when that happens.

A recent life path has led me to a new friend and co worker, Diana Larson, crochet artist extraordinaire. While sharing the quilt top with her, design magic happened. One of her beautiful snowflakes floated from a display tree to the quilt top, turning the colors of the Burgoyne blocks into the northern lights and thus the blizzard began. Twenty-five snowflakes swirled from the tree to the quilt top.

A cell phone camera allowed Judy a whole four hours to decide how to quilt it before I delivered BURGOYNE BLIZZARD to her house on the appointed day (and yes, she is still speaking to me). This quilt is a testament to her extraordinary ability to read a quilt and instinctively add quilting to enhance the design.

Once quilted and bound it was my task to finish sewing down the snowflakes. I thought "Easy, I will just add a bead or two here and there." This was the first opportunity for Judy to use that baseball bat but she let me down. Approximately 5,000 beads later, the quilt was complete.

This project represents the best of the quiltmaking experience. BRILLIANT BLIZZARD combines the design, piecing and quilting talents of old friends and the generous sharing of ability of a new friend, to make a new quilt from old blocks.

Technique

My mind works best using the triangle known in the quilting world as the 45-degree kaleidoscope triangle. The center starburst begins with an eight-pointed star constructed using my own strip piecing techniques and my Mary Sue's Triangle Ruler®.

The strips were pieced to create a diamond shape with a checkerboard design to echo the small squares in the Burgoyne Surrounded block. Once the necessary strips were cut and pieced in the proper order (fig. 1), all that

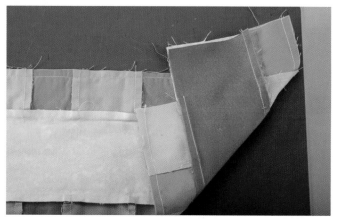

Fig. 1.

was necessary was to lay the ruler on the pieced unit and cut eight easily pieced diamonds to create the star points (fig. 2). In all there are 36 pieced diamonds with varying color placement. The most difficult part of the process was making sure the colors ended up where I wanted them.

Fig. 2.

Kaleidoscope triangles were sewn on each side of the pieced diamond, creating a large Kaleidoscope triangle, and so on until eight large 45-degree triangles are constructed, each containing two rows of pieced diamonds. I chose to piece these triangles used in the second star row to completely surround the center star. The eight triangles are then sewn together in pairs, pairs into halves, halves into a whole octagon forming the star circle. Large right triangles sewn to alternating corners turned the octagon into a square for easy manageability.

The border is created by piecing three quarters of a Burgoyne Surrounded block for each corner and inserting a large Kaleidoscope triangle unit, pieced like the center units, in the center of each border. Bang! There is the star on top of the Burgoyne Surrounded blocks.

Judy chose to use two layers of batting in the project, a base layer of cotton and a silk top layer to create some loft. The snowflakes were temporarily secured for the quilting process, and later beaded to secure them for posterity.

Burgoyne Surrounded Block

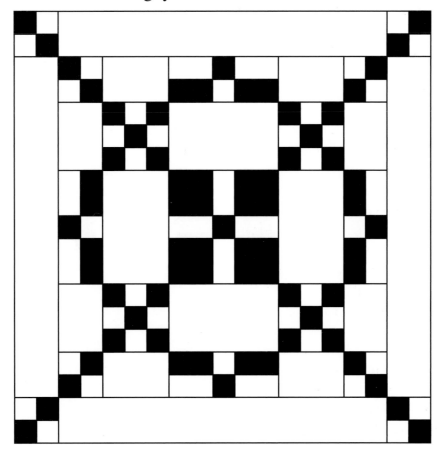

The National Quilt Museum

The National Quilt Museum is the world's largest and foremost museum devoted to quilts and the only museum dedicated to today's quilts and quiltmakers. Established in 1991 by American Quilter's Society founders Bill and Meredith Schroeder as a not-for-profit organization, the museum is located in a 27,000 square foot facility in Paducah, Kentucky. It was designed specifically to exhibit quilts effectively and safely. Three expansive galleries envelop visitors in color, exquisite stitchery, and design and feature ten to twelve exhibits annually.

In July 2008, the United States Congress designated the Museum of the American Quilter's Society as The National Quilt Museum of the United States. While the designation does not come with federal funding, it provides national recognition of the museum's significance and stature as a national cultural and educational treasure.

The highlight of any visit is The William & Meredith Schroeder Gallery with a rotating exhibit of quilts from the museum's collections of over 300 quilts. The nucleus of the collection is composed of extraordinary contemporary quilts collected privately by the Schroeders and donated to the museum. The collection continues to expand with the addition of purchase award quilts from the annual AQS Quilt Show & Contest and with the additions by purchase or donation of exceptional quilts selected to enhance the collection. In 2006, Oh Wow!—a stunning collection of more than 40 miniature quilts—was added to the collection.

Educational programs offered in three well-equipped classrooms serve local and national audiences. The museum offers an annual schedule of in-depth workshops taught by master quilters. Educational activities are also offered for youth including hands-on activities, summer quilt camps, and the School Block Challenge. Exhibitions like New Quilts from an Old Favorite, which are developed by

Photo by Jessica Byassee

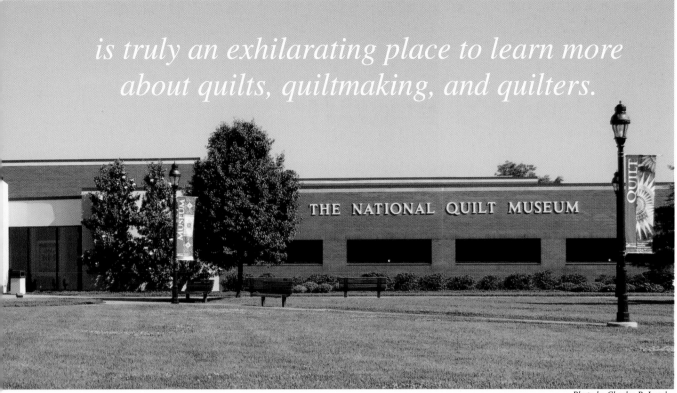

is truly an exhilarating place to learn more about quilts, quiltmaking, and quilters.

the museum, travel to other galleries and museums, helping to educate and inspire a wider spectrum of viewers.

With more than 800 quilt-related book titles available, the museum's bookstore has one of the largest selections of quilt books anywhere. In addition, the museum's shop offers quilts and quilt-related merchandise as well as fine crafts by artisans from the region and beyond. The entire facility is wheelchair accessible.

Located at 215 Jefferson Street in historic downtown Paducah, Kentucky, the museum is open year-round 10 am to 5 pm, Monday through Saturday. Check the museum's Web site, www.quiltmuseum.org,

Teacher Pat Holly with workshop student. Photo by Jessica Byassee.

for extended hours during special events. Museum programs and events can also be found on the Web site. For more information, e-mail info@quiltmuseum. org, call 270-442-8856, or write to The National Quilt Museum, PO Box 1540, Paducah, Kentucky 42002-1540.

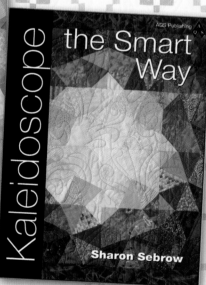